"I gotta say, this is an awesome perspective for men to consider as well! We often don't realize the collateral damage our choices cost our families. This perspective inspires me to a more vigilant effort on behalf of the woman who has chosen to risk her future with me. I plan to read this aloud with my wife. It will strengthen our understanding of our relationship and where we take it from here."

—Bryan Duncan, recording artist and singer-songwriter

"Tina Samples, this time along with her husband, Dave, has done it again! *Messed Up Men of the Bible* is a fascinating and informative read. It reminds readers of all the 'messed up' men that God used throughout Scripture. We shouldn't be surprised that God uses the imperfect among us, though. Who else has He ever had to work with?"

—Martha Bolton, former staff writer for Bob Hope, playwright, and author of 88 books, including *Josiah for President*

"At one time in my life, I felt messed up and beyond hope. It was when I began to see my life from the Lord's perspective that He was able to begin cleaning up the mess I had made. Tina and Dave have taken episodes of messed up men of the Bible and revealed how God meets us right where we are but loves us enough not to leave us there. With clarity and vivid storytelling, they have written a book that beautifully illustrates just how amazing God is at cleaning up the messes we make of our lives and at the same time shows how able our God is to redeem and love us into our true callings. My takeaway? I see others differently and more hopefully now—and am able to see that our God wastes nothing! Reading these stories emboldens me to seek to be a man after God's own heart."

—Dennis Jernigan, husband, father, grandfather, worshiper, song receiver, and author of the autobiography *Sing Over Me*

"The Bible is brutally honest when it comes to the flaws and failures of God's great leaders, and Tina and Dave Samples, with transparency and authenticity, bring hope and encouragement to women with 'messed up men' in their lives, and men seeking to make a message out of a mess. Delightful, informative, and inspirational—this book is perfect to read on your own, with your spouse, or with a group!"

—Rebecca Ashbrook Carrell, morning show cohost on 90.9 KCBI, blogger, and author of *Holy Jellybeans: Finding God Through Everyday Things*

"This book belongs on the nightstand of every wife who is searching her heart for answers. *Messed Up Men of the Bible* is woven with hard-won wisdom on how to love the messed up men in our lives with grace, courage, and compassion. Dave and Tina Samples have carefully adorned this valuable resource with practical tips, sage advice, and biblical stories that help us bring forth the purpose and potential in the men we love. Best of all, this book returns our fixation to God, the only one powerful enough to transform a wounded man into a warrior. My hope is that *Messed Up Men of the Bible* helps women be the kind and gentle spirits men need us to be as they battle through the trials of life, and that some day our men will look back and say, 'It was *her* faith that inspired me to change for the better.'"

—Jennifer Strickland, former professional model, inspirational speaker, founder of URMore.org, and author of *Beautiful Lies* and *More Beautiful Than You Know*

"This is a wonderful book and study guide! Dave and Tina tag team to create a bridge between various men of the Bible, with their 'messed up' issues, and today's men, who essentially face the same strengths and obstacles. This is a very encouraging, hopeful, and practical guide for letting Christ bring us to a place of understanding and maturity in our walk with Him and each other. There is a great weaving of personal stories, biblical accounts, and timely truth-filled commentary, helping us make sense of it all."

—Jeff Nelson, producer and worship leader

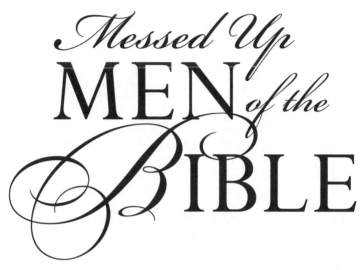

Messed Up MEN of the BIBLE

Seeing the Men in Your Life Through God's Eyes

Tina Samples & Dave Samples

Kregel
Publications

ISBN 978-0-8254-4383-1

Printed in the United States of America
16 17 18 19 20 21 22 23 24 25 / 5 4 3 2 1

For Dad.
I'm so thankful the messes didn't define you.
I praise God for changing your life. Can't wait to see you.
I love you always.

For Mom.
Thank you for what you taught me, for your example,
and for allowing me to tell our story.
I love you always.
—Tina

Dedicated to Mom and Dad.
I'm grateful for your sacrifice, your example,
your faith, and your love.
—David

Contents

Introduction **9**

1 **Peter** A Double-Minded Man **15**

2 **Nebuchadnezzar** A Conceited King **29**

3 **Saul** A Reckless Ruler **42**

4 **Moses** A Destructive Deliverer **58**

5 **Job** A Sick Soul **74**

6 **Elijah** A Pitiful Prophet **89**

7 **Solomon** A Wayward Worshiper **105**

8 **David** A Failing Father **119**

9 **Judas** A False Friend **136**

10 **Samson** A Lustful Leader **152**

11 **The Demoniac** An Oppressed Outcast **167**

12 **Gideon** A Weak-Kneed Warrior **181**

Conclusion **197**

Notes **203**

Acknowledgments **207**

About the Authors **211**

A Message from Tina & Dave **213**

Introduction

TINA ❧ In Job, it says, "Man is born for trouble, as sparks fly upward" (Job 5:7). We women have seen sparks fly upward, around, and upside down. We've seen the spark of love that ignites the beating of a heart and the spark of pain that stops it. We know the trouble we've had with man, and man with us. Even Adam and Eve understood that word, *trouble*. Yet we can't seem to live without men. How many men are in your life? Boss, employee, coworker, grandfather, father, brother, uncle, close friend, dating partner, spouse, son? I've been surrounded by men my whole life. I grew up with eight brothers, married Dave, and had two sons. Even our dog is a male! Yes, there is too much testosterone flying around my house.

Having so many men in my life allowed me to experience male and female personality differences firsthand. Some men in my life remain quiet and keep their hearts tucked in deep places. Others open their chests, place their hearts on the table, and let it all out. I must say, I love men who do that. I'm not talking sappy moments but transparent moments; moments when a man risks it all to openly share his heart.

In high school I had more male than female friends. Yes, I was one of those girls. For some reason guys came to me with their problems. In high school the issues were all about girls, dating, and love, but college shed a different light. Men struggled with homosexuality, abuse, controlling parents, their value, purpose, addictions, and guilt.

Long ago I realized that men are just trying to figure out who they are and what they want out of life. Sound familiar? Women want the same. That task in itself is huge; without God in the center, it's almost impossible to achieve.

I spent my honeymoon at an amusement park. Okay, I could have become a little upset about that one, but due to finances and our love for roller coasters, my husband thought an amusement park was a good idea. Sometimes men have a difficult time figuring women out. There were no fancy restaurants, and my hotel room wasn't adorned with fresh rose petals. My vision of softly glowing candles flickering in the room was just that—a vision. Yet even though our brief trip wasn't my idea of a luxurious honeymoon, our time playing together was joyous.

(Allow me to press the *pause* button and give my husband the shout-out he deserves. Twenty years later, he did take me on the honeymoon I never had—a lavish cruise to the Caribbean. Thank you, honey.)

Before long we had two sons and shared our love for the amusement park with them. But over time, I developed a fear of heights. One memorable day at the park impacted me in a profound way. Here's what happened.

"Okay, last ride call," said my husband. My oldest son decided he wanted to ride the Mind Eraser with me since I didn't get to ride it earlier.

I went through my symptoms of pulse racing, hands sweating, and head swimming. I was afraid. On the way up to the Mind Eraser, I asked, "Jaren, what can I expect from this ride?"

My eight-year-old son said, "Well, your head is going to bob this way and that way. We go up, around, and upside down. You lose your mind—but it only lasts three seconds."

I lose my mind? "Oh, give me strength, Lord," I mumbled. I sat in the seat, my heart sprinting—and I whined. I whined like a little baby. Out loud. "I can't do this!"

"Just close your eyes, Mom!" my son said as we buckled up. Something was wrong with this picture.

My son showed me how to buckle up, told me not to look down, and advised me to close my eyes. *How old am I?* Where had the mother in me gone? I looked over the edge for just a moment and reality hit. I was going to die.

"I can't do this!" I bellowed. At that moment, the coaster took off at high speed. My feet dangled in midair. I thought my shoes might fly across the park and hit some poor elderly woman in the head.

I shut my eyes tight, and, just like my son warned, my head bobbed this way and that as if it had a mind of its own. Pain pounded in my ears. I screamed and screamed. *What happened to the three seconds?* I tried to yell "Help!" but couldn't get even that much out intelligibly. I'm sure drool dripped down my chin.

And then I heard a voice from afar, piercing through the hundred-mile-an-hour rumble of the coaster wheels: "Mom! Press your head firmly into the headrest!"

What? What was that?

Again: "Mom! Press—your—head—firmly—into—the—headrest!"

A miracle! How did my son know I needed to do that? The seats were positioned so no one could see the person next to them due to the padding on the sides. Jaren must have seen my head bobbing out in front.

I immediately obeyed. I pressed my head firmly into the headrest, and with it came great relief. My head stopped bobbing, my body stabilized, and I felt more secure. Fear eased and the pain ceased because I wasn't knocking myself out. In a few seconds we came to a stop and coasted into the area where others awaited their turn. After unsticking my eyelashes from squeezing my eyes so tight, I looked up. I was alive! I patted my limbs—*yes. I'm here.* I beamed at my genius and generous son, who thought of nothing more than taking care of his mom.

Our lives are very much like that moment. Riding through life with a messed up man can feel as if we're on the biggest coaster in the world. Our feet dangle midair and we feel tossed and tattered. Through twists and turns, even spinning upside down at times, we scream, "Help! I can't do this!" But oh, my friends, there is a voice calling in the chaos, trying to break through the sound barrier. You second-guess yourself: *What is that? What did I hear?* He calls again. The voice sounds and feels like it's coming from a distance, but just as with my son calling to me from the next seat, the voice is actually coming from right beside you.

God sits with us. He encourages the faint of heart: "You can do it! It's okay!"

Relationships can be messy and difficult, especially when you're living with a messed up man. Trying to maneuver through life without losing your mind can feel overwhelming. When you find yourself on rough terrain, and when life feels as if it's spiraling out of control, listen to the voice. Listen to God shout, "Press your head firmly into the headrest."

His rest. In *Him*. The Bible says that in Him we find rest. In Christ we find stability, peace, and security to handle any ride ahead, especially with the messed up man in our life. And when we approach the ride as it should be ridden, it is exciting, enjoyable, and exhilarating. So get ready. Strap in. It's go time.

DAVE 🦊 This is not a book on how to fix your messed up man. It's bigger than that. This is a book about how to join God in His mission of transforming your man to fit into God's perfect plan and place. It is a hope-filled book overflowing with messed up men who had messy lives. Ironically, these were the kinds of men God chose to use for His great purposes and achievements. From their examples, you can learn how to live in a healthy way with your own messed up man. I know because I am one such man—messed up through and through.

Within these chapters, you will hear some of my stories, my struggles, and yes, even my successes. I see myself in so many of the biblical men. The point for you is not merely to discover that your man has much in common with the weaknesses of biblical men; more important, it is to see that he, like the men of the Bible, can rise above his man-made mess and fulfill his God-given destiny. This book is not as much about the messed up man in your life as it is about God opening your eyes to see that man differently—with infinitely more potential—than you see him now.

You will read incredible stories of men who are not superheroes or spiritual giants but simple men, lacking in many areas yet still used mightily by God. You'll read about Peter, who had a hard time living consistently, one moment speaking for God and the next serving as a mouthpiece of Satan. You'll find that King David, the writer of most of the Psalms, was a lousy dad. You'll have a heart-to-heart moment with Gideon, who lacked courage, and you'll see how Nebuchadnezzar struggled with pride. Somewhere in these pages you will recognize the man in your life.

This book covers men who deal with anger, depression, and chronic illness. We will take a closer look at sexual integrity, at integrity in general, and at men who have a difficult time becoming the spiritual leaders of their homes.

At the end of each chapter, you will find a section called "Moving Beyond the Mess" for personal or group use. You can even sit with a friend and work through it over a warm cup of tea. And if your man is willing, what an amazing journey you can have when you work through it together!

My friends, be encouraged. God chooses to use messed up men. Their weaknesses, failures, and frailties are waiting to be transformed into promise and potential. Don't give up on your man before he becomes God's miracle. In the process, you might find a miracle within yourself.

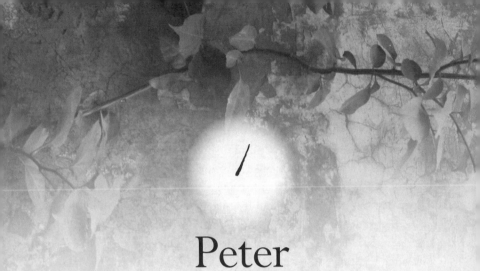

Peter

A Double-Minded Man

No good thing does He withhold from
those who walk uprightly.
PSALM 84:11

Betty twisted in the oversized chair, leaned into her husband's words, and clenched her jaw. One ear clung to his assurances while the other turned away; one part of her chose trust while the other fought to believe. She felt split down the middle.

Her mind drifted to moments when she had accepted his every sentence without hesitation, suspicion, or fear. She recalled never having reason to doubt his words or deeds. But as the years of their marriage progressed, she stumbled upon "little white lies"—minimized issues, storytelling, and broken truths.

Each lie thickened the glass wall separating the relationship. Betty wondered when the glass might finally shatter. He had done it so often now—inconsistencies in behavior and speech, pretending to be something he wasn't. Who was this man? How could she find confidence in him? Could the relationship be restored?

TINA ❧ Do you identify with Betty's story? I remember as a small girl losing confidence in my father's words. My moments of excitement at the thought of going somewhere or doing something with my dad were cruelly crushed when those plans fell to the ground. My father's inconsistent lifestyle failed to bring something a little girl needed—stability.

My dad was a huge mess, and his inconsistency weakened his character. He struggled with an alcohol addiction that led him to live an unpredictable lifestyle. When sober, he was caring and compassionate, but when he drank, he was cruel and unkind. Which of the two characters was my real father?

That is a question many women ask about the messed up man in their life: "Who are you?"

Women want to believe in their fathers as well as the other men in their lives. When fathers struggle with being authentic, they leave muddy footprints on little girls' hearts. We then grow up and enter relationships with messed up men who also struggle.

Chuck Colson said, "We must be the same person in private and in public. Only the Christian worldview gives us the basis for this kind of integrity."[1] But are we ever the same person in public that we are in private?

Men lacking authenticity isn't something new in today's world—even Jesus walked with those who struggled with honesty.

Six Signs Someone Might Lack Authenticity

1. They behave differently in different crowds.
2. They aren't completely transparent. They may tell the truth but not the whole truth.
3. They change their values to fit others.
4. They are unstable and shaky when it comes to standing up for their Christian beliefs.
5. They are easily manipulated by others and make unhealthy compromises.
6. They often focus on self.

Wooden Sticks and Steel Rods

DAVE ❧ The apostle Peter is a man not unlike the men in your life. At times he attempts to be more than he is—more spiritual, more confident, more successful. Peter wants to be the best he can, but like all men, he isn't quite there. He teeter-totters between right and wrong. Let's look at a few examples.

In Matthew 16, Jesus asks a simple question: "Who do people say that the Son of Man is?" Peter's spot-on answer, "You are the Christ, the Son of the living God," is met with Jesus's approval. Jesus responds, "Blessed are you, Simon Barjona, because flesh and blood did not reveal this to you, but My Father who is in heaven" (vv. 13–17).

Yet just six verses later, Peter receives Jesus's stern rebuke, "Get behind Me, Satan! You are a stumbling block to Me; for you are not setting your mind on God's interests, but man's."

The rebuke comes after Peter, alarmed at Jesus's prediction of His own impending death in Jerusalem, attempts to correct Jesus. In response, Jesus rebukes Peter for giving voice to Satan. Isn't that amazing! One moment, Peter is speaking the divine words of the Father; the very next, he is speaking the lying words of Satan.

Perhaps you've seen this in the men close to you. Sometimes they are brilliant and spiritual. But at other times, they seem filled with deceit and anything but God's words.

Paul relates another incident of Peter's inconsistency:

> When Cephas came to Antioch, I opposed him to his face, because he stood condemned. For prior to the coming of certain men from James, he used to eat with the Gentiles; but when they came, he began to withdraw and hold himself aloof, fearing the party of the circumcision. The rest of the Jews joined him in hypocrisy, with the result that even Barnabas was carried away by their hypocrisy. But when I saw that they were not straightforward about the truth of the gospel, I said to Cephas in the presence of all, "If you, being a Jew, live like the Gentiles and not like the Jews, how is it that you compel the Gentiles to live like Jews?" (Gal. 2:11–14)

Paul publicly condemned Peter for behaving one way around the Gentile believers and another around Jewish believers. We often call this inconsistent behavior a lack of integrity or lack of authenticity. Merriam-Webster defines *authentic*, the word from which *authenticity* derives, as "real or genuine . . . not false or imitation . . . true to one's own personality, spirit, or character."[2]

A steel rod is stronger than a wooden stick. The stick is no less authentic than the rod; it just has a different kind of authenticity. The stick has the authenticity of wood while the rod has the authenticity of steel. But what if the stick tried to pose as a steel rod? The stick would be pretending to be something it is not. It does not have the same strength or qualities as steel and will not hold up under the same pressures.

Now let's look at the man in your life. If your messed up man tries to pose as something other than what he is, he lacks authenticity. Perhaps the man you believed to be steel has broken or is breaking under pressures that a wooden stick cannot possibly support. Peter experienced brokenness when his words shifted from a faith-filled confession to fear-filled caution. He was again broken when Paul confronted his shift in something as simple as food and drink. Is your man less than or other than who he says he is? Are there honesty issues in his life?

Here's the good news: your messed up man is in the company of a great many biblical heroes, including Peter. You may have experienced the consequences of leaning on a stick that couldn't support you the way you expected. The truth is, no human can ever support you fully. Only God can have that place in your life.

TINA ⚜ I'm sitting here asking myself if I view Dave as a stick or an iron rod. Okay, I won't answer that, but looking back, I clearly remember the stick breaking a time or two. Yet, I also remember my husband's firm grasp on me and his family, grasps that could not be loosened or torn asunder. He was an iron rod in iron cladding. And oh, how it melted my thick, scared walls as security brushed over me. Kind of like butter on a hot bun.

What *is* his true character? Sometimes men are inconsistent in their behaviors, actions, and ways of living. Of course, women are too. Perhaps some men, like some women, struggle to find authenticity, genuineness, and truthfulness, or to live a life consistent with who they really are.

Circumstances may play a role in a man's authenticity. Abraham told Sarah to pretend to be his sister in order to save his own life. Jacob's sons pretended to be one thing in front of their father and another to their brother, Joseph, whom they threw into a pit and sold into slavery. Were they loving and concerned brothers or jealous bullies?

When reading about Peter, we ponder the question, "Who are you?" Are you courageous or cowardly, a lover or fighter, a friend or foe, a Jew or Gentile, fearless or fearful, a believer or an unbeliever? Peter struggled with all of these matters. Authenticity is about being consistent with who one is.

Life is filled with decisions, and though we would like to help the men in our life make decisions, and good ones, that isn't our responsibility. Still, we try by picking out Sunday clothes, discouraging ice-cream runs, and distracting them while they pass by favorite fast-food restaurants. Who reminds them to get off their phones for family time, or that the doctor said not to do *that* because this *would* happen? Sometimes men don't do a very good job of making decisions, and we've experienced time and again how their bad decisions have impacted their lives. (Of course, we women have the same issue.)

Peter came to a point where his bad decision created a moment of weakness and failure. Jesus knew Peter would fail. Jesus didn't keep it a secret either; he told Peter he would fail. Can you imagine? How would it feel to have Jesus look you square in the eye and tell you when and how you're going to fail?

The moment arrived, a moment requiring a huge decision for Peter. Would he be authentic or not? Would he boldly declare who he really was—or hide it?

Now Peter was sitting outside in the courtyard, and a servant-girl came to him and said, "You too were with Jesus the Galilean." But he denied it before them all, saying, "I do not know what you are talking about." When he had gone out to the gateway, another servant-girl saw him and said to those who were there, "This man was with Jesus of Nazareth." And again he denied it with an oath, "I do not know the man." A little later the bystanders came up and said to Peter, "Surely you too are one of them; for even the way you talk gives you away." Then he began to curse and swear, "I do not know the man!" And immediately a rooster crowed. And Peter remembered the word which Jesus had said, "Before a rooster crows, you will deny Me three times." And he went out and wept bitterly. (Matt 26:69–75)

Can we attest to moments of blowing it? I'm not a very good cook. One day, while my husband and I worked upstairs in our home offices, I heard a loud pop. The pop sounded like a gun. We both jumped up and ran downstairs. I turned toward the kitchen and found our lab looking up at the stove, tail wagging as if to say, "Up there!" Upon further investigation, I realized I forgot that I had put eggs in a pot to boil. My forgetfulness created an unfolding of events that ultimately led to eggs exploding. Fragments of egg were everywhere! In my attempt to fix the situation, I grabbed the scalding pot and thrust it under cold water. My husband yelled, "No!"

You guessed it. When the water hit the eggs, those that hadn't already burst exploded at that very moment. Shrapnel of egg hit me square in the face, speckled my hair, and splattered my clothes. I stood dumbfounded—frozen as if I really were hit by shrapnel. I expected my husband to do what I felt Jesus would have done—grab a towel and help clean me up. Instead, he stood there, lips curled and eyebrows raised, and said, "You have egg on your face."

Isn't that what we often do when the men in our life mess up? Peter's embarrassment before the Lord was a gut-wrenching moment; a moment of recognition and realization. Sometimes our messes lead to those moments; sometimes they leave us broken and weeping—or at the very least, with egg on our faces.

Undeserved Grace

When moving, my family often stayed in old, abandoned homes. One particular home stands out in my mind, not because of its age but because of an incident that affected me in the house. My parents made arrangements to run to the grocery store, but before leaving, they warned us kids, "Whatever you do, don't go upstairs." The stairs were rotten, unsteady, and dangerous. (The fire department burned down the house a short time after we moved out because a young teen died going up those steps.)

After Mom and Dad left, my younger sister and I looked up the steps as if looking up a huge mountain. Perhaps hidden treasures lingered above! We had to find out. Boards creaked and cracked ominously with each step. Holding each other's hand tightly, we kept climbing, side-stepping holes here and there.

Reaching the top felt like summiting Everest. Our feet shuffled down the hallway to the first room. Tense with anticipation, we peered in. Nothing. The empty room stared back at us. Each room resembled the previous.

Except the last one. A turn of the knob, and we stepped inside to find an old calendar hanging forlornly on the wall. The large image of Jesus caused our hearts to leap. Taking the calendar off the grimy wall, we cautiously made our way back downstairs and carried it around the rest of the afternoon.

Our excitement came to a halt when we heard the rumble of a vehicle pulling into the driveway. Squealing and shrieking, we scampered to find the perfect hiding spot for our treasure. Then we went off to play and forgot all about it—until . . .

"Tina! Tina and Pam!"

My mother's tone could raise the hair on a pig's back. We froze, our beating hearts pounding in our ears. One more call loosened our legs, and we ran like the wind to her.

"Did you go upstairs?" she asked, brows creased and lips pursed.

We shook our heads. "No ma'am. We didn't go up the stairs."

There was a silent pause. And that's when I noticed the haze in the kitchen, with smoke wafting up toward the ceiling. Perhaps my sister and I had made a bad decision in hiding the calendar in the oven.

Our mother asked again, "Did you go upstairs?"

Caught. I opened my mouth and let the truth stumble out. I don't recall all my words, but I remember saying, "We just wanted Jesus."

My sister and I tensed and waited for the spanking of our lives. But something unexpected happened. There in the center of that smoke-filled, dirty kitchen, our mother dropped to her knees in front of us. Crying, she scooped us up in her arms and, pulling our dirty cheeks next to her wet face, she prayed. Her body trembled against ours. I don't remember her words, but I'll never forget her love and grace. Her embrace—and God's.

A few years back, I asked Mom if she remembered what she prayed over us that day. She said, "I prayed you would come to know the real Jesus." We did—and I became a pastor's wife, and my sister became a missionary.

There's nothing like big arms pulling a scared body into a warm, graceful hug. My mother's embrace made me want to become more truthful with her, more consistent in walking a path of good and godly character. And that's how it is with God and our messed up men. Whether we like it or not, or feel the man in our life deserves it, God embraces him.

Men fear the reactions of women, what we will think of them if we ever discover their lack of authenticity, and what that discovery might do to the relationship. Our own hurtful emotions as women get in the way of handing out undeserved embraces.

It isn't the fault of women that men struggle. The question is, how can women embrace men during those vulnerable moments when men work to build honest character? How can we provide safe places for men to dwell in while God opens their eyes and hearts so they can become more like Him?

Peter failed Jesus. But Peter would later learn that Jesus takes the towel and wipes egg off our faces, picks us up, and embraces us—even in the midst of our failures.

The Secret to Peter's Success

How do you picture Peter? I picture him as a strong, brawny man. When I look at the men in my family (and there are many), I envision Peter. I think of Peter as rough around the edges, maybe not up on his people skills, and not a frequent bather. I picture him as someone who loved the outdoors and fishing, and who spent too much time away from his family working and playing—a man who loved adventure. I think of someone who didn't always watch his language, acting one way in a crowd and quite another when out with the boys; as not always balanced in life and perhaps not always doing a good job of being the man of his home. Does that sound familiar?

While Peter's wife is unnamed in Scripture, Peter's writings give us a glimpse of her character. In 1 Peter 3:1–6, Peter addresses women. It's odd what he says to us: "Wives, in the same way submit yourselves to your own husbands so that, if any of them do not believe the word, they may be won over without words by the behavior of their wives, when they see the purity and reverence of your lives" (NIV).

Peter is saying to women, "You are more likely to change the messed up man in your life by your behavior than by your words." It's the old saying: "You can catch more flies with honey than with vinegar." I can see your lips curve as I write. Those of you who sway the man in your life with honey know what I'm talking about. Men are influenced by the women in their circle. Men learn about women through their grandmothers, aunts, sisters, moms, dating partners, friends, and wives. Men learn about women not only from what men say about them and what they observe on the streets but also, and very importantly, from their interactions with women. Our lifestyle is a testament to men of what we believe.

But let's get real. Wouldn't it be nice to walk around the house with a perfect attitude? It's hard to do that, though, when our man doesn't fulfill our desires. We want consistency in helping around the house and caring for the children. We want our man to be where he says he will be and do what he says he will do. Who's tired of "I'll do it tomorrow"? A man's inconsistency throws a trip wire right in the middle of our best attitudes. I've stubbed my toe and stumbled over my husband's words more times than I can count. I imagine multitudes of women walking around with bandaged toes. Our feet hurt!

So how did Peter's wife walk through life with him? Again, little is said of her in the Scriptures. There is, however, this vital point: she traveled with her husband.[3] And that is a huge testament to how she felt about Peter. Imagine how difficult it would be to roam the countryside with the man in your life if you didn't respect and admire him or his work. Conclusion: Peter's wife must have *believed in* and *supported* Peter.

Peter goes on to say that we will win over our messed up men not only with our behavior but also "when they see the purity and reverence of [our] lives" (1 Peter 3:2 NIV). Was Peter's wife the perfect example of this? In the midst of Peter's failures, did she continue to show her love by her actions and behavior? Did she continue to show Peter purity and reverence (*reverence* meaning "honor or respect that is felt for or shown to [someone or something]"[4])? Wow! I need to meet Peter's wife!

Then again, Peter's wife could have been a nagging woman whose sole purpose of traveling with him was to make his life miserable. We don't really know. Peter could have written this entire chapter with that kind of wife in mind!

Peter continues, "Your beauty should not come from outward adornment. . . . Rather, it should be that of your inner self, the unfading beauty of a gentle and quiet spirit, which is of great worth in God's sight" (vv. 3–4 NIV). We know Peter's wife could have expressed her thoughts about his lack of integrity loud and clear (and maybe she did), but perhaps she did as Peter wrote. Though Peter may have deserved a tongue-lashing at times, maybe his wife radiated the "unfading beauty of a gentle and quiet spirit." Peter understood the value of that; he said it "is of great worth in God's sight."

How do men understand the value of what women can give them? How do men understand anything from women unless men experience it? Suppose Peter knew how it felt to be treated with a gentle and quiet spirit, and with a behavior that could win him over to change his life. Suppose he understood the value of these things because he received them. What if, in addressing how women and men should treat one another, Peter wrote not only from the wisdom and guidance of the Holy Spirit but also from personal familiarity?

I used to run around the house saying, "This is not a mess—not a mess," but now I find myself saying, "Gentle and quiet spirit, Tina. Gentle and quiet spirit." I don't always get it right, but I am trying to remind myself when to hold my tongue and when to speak the truth in love.

That kind of character does not go unnoticed by God or by the man in your life. That kind of character has significance. And it carries a huge price tag. The word *worth* (as in, "of great worth in God's sight") is translated "precious" in the Greek and has the same meaning as in Mark 14: "There came a woman with an alabaster vial of *very costly* perfume of pure nard" (v. 3, emphasis mine). The perfume was priceless. And according to Peter, our gentle and quiet spirit is just as valuable in God's eyes. It is precious.

In my life, there have been times I spoke when I should have been silent; times I addressed an issue when I should have left it alone; times I tried to fix something that wasn't mine to fix. So I look not only at Peter's words, but also into the life of his wife, a woman whose name I do not know, in order to envision what she may have been like. Perhaps part of Peter's writing to women traces to one simple truth: Peter's wife understood who Peter really was.

Light Meets Dark

DAVE ❧ Imagine Peter's despair as he attempts to get on with his life. The events of the past few days are confusing at best: the betrayal, the crucifixion, the empty tomb. I can relate to Peter's shame and guilt as he plays over in his mind a hundred times the unfortunate decisions he made. How do you deny someone you love so much? How do you get so self-centered that you violate everything you believe in? I don't understand it, but I've done it. And likely your own messed up man has failed as well, whether he talks about it or not.

John describes a beautiful picture of restoration in the final chapter of his gospel. Reading chapter 21 is worth your time before we continue. I'll wait . . .

Have you read it? Good. Let's summarize. Peter and the boys are fishing. It has been a long night of fruitless casts, but they are doing the thing they do best. Fishing often involves thinking, talking, laughing, dreaming, sometimes even crying. That's the scene when we hear the Savior's voice echo across the waters from the shore: "Hey, boys, you're not having any luck, are you? Maybe try the other side of the boat." They cast their net once more, and this time they find the mother lode. John understands and yells, "It's the Lord!" Peter dives in and swims for shore. Soon laughter explodes around a campfire breakfast, just like a hundred times before.

Jesus takes Peter aside and asks him three times (perhaps revisiting Peter's painful threefold betrayal), "Do you love me?" Buried in the Greek text is an interesting truth. You may already know that the Greek language in which the New Testament was written includes more than one word for love. When Jesus asks Peter in John 21:15, "Do you love Me more than these?" the Greek word used is *agapeo*, which is a sacrificial kind of love. Peter responds, "Yes, Lord; you know that I love You." But the word for "love" in Peter's response is *phileo*, meaning "brotherly love" (as in Philadelphia, "City of Brotherly Love"). The question and answer are repeated a second time in verse 16, using the same Greek words as in verse 15: "Do you *agapeo* Me?" "Yes, Lord, you know that I *phileo* you." In verse 17 we find the third exchange with a slight change of wording. Jesus asks, "Do you *phileo* Me?" Peter is grieved because Jesus has asked the third time, "Do you love [*phileo*] Me?" And Peter said to Him, "Lord, You know all things; You know that I love [*phileo*] You."

Let me suggest that in the same way that Peter's three denials of Jesus revealed his lack of integrity, the answers to these three love questions reveal Peter's restoration of integrity: in other words, getting honest with himself and with Jesus. Peter boasted that he would be willing to die with Jesus. That boast proved to be a broken wooden stick. Peter now understands and accepts his own weakness as the place where he really is. He really does love Jesus—just not enough to die for Him. At least, not yet. For Peter, this is where the healing begins. Jesus is meeting Peter where he's at, not where Peter wants to be. Integrity is honesty, even if it's not where we want to be. Don't worry, men; you have plenty of time to grow, but we dare not skip the honesty step. Ladies, just as Jesus embraced Peter, you too can lovingly accept your man's weakness without settling for a weak man. God wasn't finished with Peter, who would eventually die a martyr's death, demonstrating his *agapeo* love for Jesus to a watching world. Tradition tells us that Peter was crucified upside down, at his request, because he felt unworthy to die in the same way as his Lord. Your messed up man will likely find healing as well when the light meets the dark.

Tools for Helping Light Meet the Dark

Support. Support your messed up man and his work. Travel with him, work with him, and let him know what he's doing right!

Come alongside. Willingly come alongside your messed up man and encourage him to be the leader God knows he can be.

Talk less, act more. Win over your messed up man by your godly behavior and character, not by your nagging.

Be pure and reverent. Respect your messed up man. Men need to feel respected.

Listen. A gentle and quiet spirit is key.

Embrace with grace. Embrace as God does, even when you feel your messed up man doesn't deserve it. God tells us to love one another.

Pray. Keep praying! Ask God to come in and change, convict, lead, and guide your messed up man.

Wait. Women often jump into "fix" mode. Let God do His work. I promise, the results will be much better than if you act on your own impulses.

Moving Beyond the Mess

1. How would you define *authenticity*?
2. Consider what happens when men gather. It's not unusual for them to exaggerate. The fish gets bigger, and other stories improve in the telling. What is the difference between those moments and the times when a man really struggles with truthfulness?
3. Why do people in general struggle with acting the same in private as in public?
4. Read back through the first few verses of 1 Peter 3. How can Peter's writings help a woman live with a man who struggles to live a consistent life? How can she encourage her man in this area?
5. Take a look at Paul's authenticity. Read 2 Corinthians 1:12. What was the secret to his success in how he conducted himself?
6. *Moving to a healthier place:* What practical steps can women take that will help them move beyond a man's moments of lacking authenticity? See these verses for guidance: Ps. 130:6; Matt. 6:8; Eph. 4:14–15; 1 Thess. 5:11; Heb. 3:13; 1 Peter 5:6–7.

---

*May you come to see your value and that what you have
to offer messed up men is priceless.*

2

Nebuchadnezzar

A Conceited King

A man's pride will bring him low,
but a humble spirit will obtain honor.
PROVERBS 29:23

King Nebuchadnezzar lay sleeping in bed, content and prosperous. Then, without warning, images and visions passed through his mind. Terrified, the king awoke and commanded all his wise men be brought before him to interpret the dream.

The magicians, enchanters, astrologers, and diviners came, but they could not interpret the king's dream. Finally Daniel entered the king's presence and listened as the king shared his disturbing vision. Could Daniel give the interpretation? Daniel paused and allowed God to bring insight. What he saw alarmed him. The king had no idea how his life was about to change. Seven long years of turmoil awaited him.

DAVE 🜚 Nebuchadnezzar was king of Babylon, the most powerful nation on earth. He had all the required ingredients to cook up a serious batch of pride. This is the same king who threw Daniel's three friends into a fiery furnace because they refused to bow down and worship a golden image. But his pride was about to cost him dearly. The king's dream revealed that his mind would be changed from the mind of a man to that of an animal, and he would live with the wild beasts among the plants of the earth till seven years passed (Dan. 4:16).

Daniel interpreted the dream and begged the king to turn from his prideful ways to avoid its fulfillment. But the king continued in his arrogance and stubborn ways. As the story continues, "Twelve months later he was walking on the roof of the royal palace of Babylon. The king reflected and said, 'Is this not Babylon the great, which I myself have built as a royal residence by the might of my power and for the glory of my majesty?'" (vv. 29–30). What a pride-filled moment as the king contemplated his personal power and majesty!

How many times do we men take credit for the work of our own hands, believing we are working harder and smarter than everyone else, and that somehow we deserve the success we have achieved? Do men struggle more with that than women?

Like Nebuchadnezzar, I have basked in my own success and declared my perceived value with only a mere hat-tip to the Creator of it all. I've been full of myself, full of my pride. And like King Nebuchadnezzar, I have stood on the brink of disaster without a worry in the world.

"While the word was in the king's mouth, a voice came from heaven, saying, 'King Nebuchadnezzar, to you it is declared: sovereignty has been removed from you'" (v. 31).

The word *sovereignty* here means the ability to rule the kingdom. The verse is startling. While the boastful words are still in the king's mouth, God takes Nebuchadnezzar's kingdom away from him. In an instant. Wow! Most of my failures have taken some time for the consequences to kick in, but I wonder if there was an instant, while the words were still in my mouth, when the Father determined—at that very moment—to strip me of my kingdom. Perhaps you have witnessed a similar kingdom-stripping with the man in your life.

"Immediately the word concerning Nebuchadnezzar was fulfilled; and he was driven away from mankind and began eating grass like cattle, and his body was drenched with the dew of heaven until his hair had grown like eagles' feathers and his nails like birds' claws" (v. 33). And here we find our hero for the next seven years—eating grass. Have you ever eaten grass? Not literally but figuratively. Upon graduation from college, my first job was as an on-air personality for a local radio station. I was swept away by the modicum of fame it provided. It seemed everyone in town knew my name, and my ego quickly expanded to match my newfound fame. I experienced a reverse of fortune a few years later when the owners of a station I was managing decided to switch formats. I was left without a job and had to learn a new career selling cars. My pride took a pounding as I struggled to make a sales quota. I went from a DJ everyone loved and respected, to a salesman who was met with suspicion. I was eating grass. Humans aren't made to eat grass. This is what "eating grass" means. When I settle for less than God's very best—it's grass. When I choose sin over obedience to God—it's grass. When I take credit for God's handiwork—it's grass. When I insist on my own way—it's grass. When we attempt to meet our own needs and see ourselves as self-sufficient—it's grass.

Listen to Isaiah: "All flesh is grass, and all its loveliness is like the flower of the field. The grass withers, the flower fades, when the breath of the Lord blows upon it; surely the people are grass. The grass withers, the flower fades, but the word of our God stands forever" (Isa. 40:6–8). In the New Testament, Peter quotes this verse to insist that we are born of eternal seed—the Word of God (1 Peter 1:23–25). We were not made to eat grass. James continues the thought: "The brother of humble circumstances is to glory in his high position; and the rich man is to glory in his humiliation, because like flowering grass he will pass away. For the sun rises with a scorching wind and withers the grass; and its flower falls off and the beauty of its appearance is destroyed; so too the rich man in the midst of his pursuits will fade away" (James 1:9–11). The arrogant rich man will be humbled. Like grass, he will pass away.

The Nature of Pride

TINA ❧ A humorous quote caught my attention the other day. It said, "Let me suggest you consider the difference between dogs and cats. The master pets a dog, and the dog wags its tail and thinks, 'He must be a god.' But the master pets his cat, and the cat purrs, shuts its eyes and thinks to itself, 'I must be a god.' Though Jesus in grace reached down to us, there is still a perverse human tendency to think like the cat!"[1]

King Nebuchadnezzar stood on the roof of his Babylonian palace, inhaled a lungful of pride, and looked down upon his masterful creation. God in His goodness had provided the king with vast blessings, yet Nebuchadnezzar closed his eyes and decided, "I must be a god." Pride takes us to such a place. C. S. Lewis said, "A proud man is always looking down on things and people: and, of course, as long as you are looking down, you cannot see something that is above you."[2] I understand how it feels to live with a prideful man, especially one who looks down from on top of the world.

How do we stay humble as God grows our ministry, work, and talents? And what do we do when pride enlarges in the men we love? We can encourage men to focus on the journey rather than the end result. When we concentrate on an outcome, we lose sight of what it took to get there. Recognizing God's work brings our focus back to Him and not self.

Pride left unchecked leads to other sins. When we look at Scripture stories related to pride, we see men starting their journeys in a reasonable place. At what point does pride seep in and become an issue?

Here are a few characteristics of pride we may recognize in the men we love (and quite possibly in ourselves):

+ Pride refuses God or God's help.
+ Pride turns toward self. It is difficult for a prideful person to focus

on anyone other than himself. Pride is self-focused, self-absorbed, and self-seeking; it is desperate to be the center of attention.

✦ Pride rejects authority. Submitting is difficult.

✦ Pride struggles with displaying the fruits of the Spirit—love, joy, peace, forbearance, kindness, goodness, faithfulness, gentleness, and self-control.

✦ Pride enlarges its territory. Pride makes the person and his surroundings seem impossibly larger than they are, causing absurd exaggerations: "Look what I did!" Everything the prideful person does is promoted as bigger and better than anything or anyone else.

I love my man. I've loved him in his strengths and in his weaknesses. I haven't always liked him, but I have always loved him. There was a moment in my husband's life when God took him from a pride-filled platform to a humble homage. It was not an easy ride.

My man excelled in everything he touched. I've asked myself, "What drove him to the rooftop?" I guess some men are driven, and mine was like that. On many occasions I've scratched my head after his prideful rumblings. His need to be noticed swept him away to a place where neither of us wish to return. Pride kept us at a distance and forced a huge barrier between us. Who knew pride could do such a thing?

The excitement, passions, and drive a man can have when filled with pride amaze me. However, the superman outlook and daredevil façade eventually faded, leaving my husband in a very lonely place. As the wife of such a man, I too felt the emptiness.

I watched God take my spouse to places he alone could never reach. I was there when he received awards and honors over others just as deserving. I witnessed God elevate him to every position he ever wanted. I sat and beamed, and at times became jealous of a man who, by asking, received every desire in his heart. Though I've seen his humble, gracious, and loving nature, I've also seen his chest swell up like a giant gorilla's.

Some of my most difficult times as a wife occurred with my husband during his most pride-filled days. Equally difficult was living with him during his most humbling days. The moments God chose to humble him were just as painful as watching him become more and more prideful.

A woman has a difficult time watching her husband struggle in anything—whether good or bad. Let me add that a wife is not always innocent in the way she handles her husband's pride or her own. Women too get caught up in the rush and boast with as much force—at times, even more. There's the mother who reminds me time and again that her son went to college on an athletic scholarship. There's the woman who boasts of her husband's new business, and the proud mom who embellishes the talents of her children—things hers can do that mine can't. A woman's boasting can swell as big as a man's. And I confess, I'm as guilty as anyone. I too sometimes find myself drenched in pride.

I love what C. S. Lewis wrote:

> Pleasure in being praised is not Pride. The child who is patted on the back for doing a lesson well, the woman whose beauty is praised by her lover, the saved soul to whom Christ says, "Well done," are pleased and ought to be. For here the pleasure lies not in what you are but in the fact that you have pleased someone you wanted (and rightly wanted) to please. The trouble begins when you pass from thinking, "I have pleased him; all is well," to thinking, "What a fine person I must be to have done it."[3]

The Fall

How did Nebuchadnezzar's pride affect his family? There is no mention of his family in Scripture, yet we can assume they felt a deep loss and perhaps even embarrassment as they, along with the townspeople, looked upon their king stumbling through the wilderness like a wild animal. Were they able to empathize with his situation, or did it make them bitter?

Though the Bible gives little account of Nebuchadnezzar's wife, I can tell you from experience that when our husbands fall, we are along for the ride. Whatever impacts the man in our life also impacts the woman in his. My heart hurts with you, my friends. If you are riding your man's downfall due to pride, then you may be despairing like these women. The man in your life might lose his job. Your family may be torn apart. The man's friends may turn away from him. Something he loved to do may be stripped from his hands. If he's an addict, he may hit rock bottom. His bad decisions can have devastating consequences. And the people in his life, however they are connected, will feel the impact. Those who shouldn't get hurt often end up hurting the most.

In the midst of the fall, we don't see restoration seeping through the dark cracks—but it is there. Restoration happens when the messed up man realizes he needs help; empathizes with those he hurt; turns from his pride-filled, sinful ways; and reaches out to God.

God is the God who sees all—nothing is hidden from Him. Though God allows us to fall, His greatest desire is to pick us up. For He is the Lord our God who takes hold of our right hand and says, "Do not fear, I will help you" (Isa. 41:13).

Releasing Freedom

When something happened to the messed up men in my life, I used to take it personally. I couldn't see God working because I was too worried about how things might impact me, my family, and others around me. I felt out of control.

The greatest need many women have is to feel secure. How do we find peace and security in all things, especially in the chaos of the messed up man in our life?

I love what Sarah Young wrote in her book, *Jesus Calling*. She wrote it as if God were speaking:

Make Me the focal point of your search for security. In your private thoughts, you are still trying to order your world so that it is predictable and feels safe. Not only is this an impossible goal, but it is also counterproductive to spiritual growth.

When your private world feels unsteady and you grip My hand
for support, you are living in conscious dependence on Me.
Instead of yearning for a problem-free life, rejoice that trouble
can highlight your awareness of My presence.[4]

What did she say? Rejoice when trouble comes your way, because
trouble can highlight your awareness of God's presence. James said
something similar about considering your trials as joy because the testing of your faith produces perseverance (James 1:2–3 NIV).

In due time, I learned that what God was doing in the messed up
men in my life didn't have to hurt me. I didn't have to let their unsettled
lives unsettle me. God can work through even our cloudiest moments.

So what happens if the man in your life experiences a fall? How do
you handle it without falling apart yourself?

Sitting across from a counselor friend, I let my burning emotions
spill out. At one point he said, "Wow—that must be difficult."

"What?" I asked.

"Carrying the burdens of all those people."

He was right. I was so worried about others—how they might be
affected, what they might think—that I didn't realize I was making
myself responsible for them. And I didn't need to be. I just needed to
give myself permission to live my own life and love them. "Don't you
think God is big enough to handle their lives?" my friend asked.

Here are six things to do when you see God working in your messed
up man's life:

1. *Don't personalize it.* If what's happening in his life has to do with
   him, don't make it about you too. He's struggling. That's difficult
   because when we are connected, his struggles impact us. Work
   through the impact of his actions and trust God to work everything out.
2. *Resist the urge to play the blame game.* "When we do that," says
   therapist Michelle Kugler, "it puts the other person on the defensive, and they are immediately resistant to taking responsibility

for the situation. As a result, any grievances you have will fall on deaf ears, and this can cause as much pain and anger as the fall from pride. Instead, empathize and show unconditional love. This will require significant help from God."[5]

3. *Stay out of the whirlwind.* It's never easy to see the man in our life struggle in anything. We want to rescue, jump in, and protect. Picture a tornado. You can either jump into the center or step out and allow God to work in the midst of it. If he falls on his face, it's going to hurt. You can empathize with his suffering, you can encourage and support him, but don't get down in the mud and wallow with him. In the words of my counselor and friend, "It's not a mess!" It may look like one, but trust that God is working in all things.

4. *Create a safe place.* We create a safe place by loving unconditionally. Let him begin to take accountability for his choices and behaviors. This doesn't mean you should minimize his actions or how you've been hurt. Once your man is able to take ownership of his mistakes and wrongdoings, he is better able to "look up," regain his sanity, and make true changes.

5. *Hand it over.* Give it to God. He can handle the chaos far better than you.

6. *Pray.* Never stop pouring out words to God on behalf of your man. We aren't holding on in an unhealthy way when we pray; we're intervening on behalf of someone we love.

God once revealed to me that I didn't have to try to fix the men in my life. God showed me that as long as they were seeking Him, God could fix them.

A New Season Awaits

DAVE ✖ Our compassionate and loving God brings us through our times of darkness, and a new dawn arises. He desires to continue his good work in us. Here's what happened to Nebuchadnezzar: "At the end of that period, I, Nebuchadnezzar, raised my eyes toward heaven and my reason returned to me, and I blessed the Most High and praised and honored Him who lives forever" (Dan. 4:34). Notice the sequence here. First, Nebuchadnezzar looked to heaven; second, his sanity returned; third, he worshiped God. He had eaten grass for seven years before he looked up. Could he have looked up earlier and saved himself some grief? I want to think so. But the good news is that God continuously waits for us to raise our eyes toward heaven.

Nebuchadnezzar next discovered that his sanity had returned. Clearly, he had previously believed that he was in control of his world, that by his own hands he had made himself king of his own kingdom. That was insanity. When we take credit for God's blessing and God's grace, we are most definitely insane. When we have our eyes anywhere other than on God, we can easily lose focus on our purpose and place.

In Luke 15:11–32, Jesus tells the story of the prodigal son, who took his inheritance and left home. He chose to leave the banquet table of his father and waste all of his money on parties and friends. Around the time he spent his last dollar, a severe famine hit. The prodigal found himself in real trouble, with no money, no friends, no family, and no work. He eventually found a job feeding pigs and was so hungry that he helped himself to their slop.

Notice what happened next. In one defining moment, like Nebuchadnezzar, "he came to his senses" (Luke 15:17). The prodigal son decided to return home, and his father gloriously restored him to his previous position.

King Nebuchadnezzar looked up, received his sanity, and then, as a natural expression of gratefulness, worshiped God. We'll never go wrong when we worship God. Worship is a clear sign of sanity. Worship is where God intended the king to be all along. But Nebuchadnezzar couldn't get to the point of worshiping God because of his ego. And so it is with us: if we believe we are the ones who have established our kingdoms, then we have no room to worship God. We're too busy worshiping ourselves.

Nebuchadnezzar's humbling led to the restoration of his kingdom to him. "At that time my reason returned to me. And my majesty and splendor were restored to me for the glory of my kingdom, and my counselors and my nobles began seeking me out; so I was reestablished in my sovereignty, and surpassing greatness was added to me" (Dan. 4:36). The king received his kingdom back. The prodigal son had his ring, his robe, and his family restored to him. And God has something for you as well. God never allows us to be broken without the promise of healing and restoration.

"Now I, Nebuchadnezzar, praise, exalt and honor the King of heaven, for all His works are true and His ways just, and He is able to humble those who walk in pride" (Dan. 4:37).

TINA ❦ Humility escorts us to the cross, while pride blocks its path. When the man in our life comes to his senses and leaves his messes at the cross, God sees, hears, and restores—just like He did Nebuchadnezzar and the prodigal son.

In Daniel 4, King Nebuchadnezzar said, "My advisers and nobles sought me out, and I was restored to my throne and became even greater than before" (v. 36 NIV). I love this verse. The king's greatest friends (and more than likely his family too) sought him out. In other words, they asked about, prayed for, and requested information on behalf of him. They did not abandon or disown him. They didn't ignore him or gloat over his failure; they remained concerned, but kept their own hearts in a good place while God worked on the king's heart. The king recognized that loyalty in his family, friends, advisers, and noblemen.

Life can beat us up. Sadly, in our churches, those with whom we've gathered, communed, and prayed, and with whom we've shared our deepest secrets, can rise up against us with a big bat in hand. It's easy for people to forget about their own messed up lives when someone else's mess-ups are dangling in front of them. What I admire about King

Nebuchadnezzar's circle is that they remained steadfast and hopeful
that one day the king would return to his proper position. Praise God
for people who step *with* us, not *on* us.

French politician Charles de Montesquieu is widely credited with
saying, "To become truly great, one has to stand with people, not above
them." Ladies, my prayer is that you will have a burning passion to
stand with the messed up men in your life, not above them (nor below
them). Let us stand *together* in love and humility, seeking God's face and
His tender care. When a woman walks through difficult seasons with
the man she loves, she too finds, in the end, great healing in her own
life. Understandably, women have a difficult time walking with someone who is walking on a rebellious path. Above all, allow God to escort
you on the right path while He continues to reach out to the messed up
men in your life.

God is a good and loving God who desires to restore. He will restore
men, just as He did Nebuchadnezzar, to the place they need to be, to
their rightful positions, if they will allow Him to do so. Pray diligently,
trusting that God will finish the good work He started in the life of the
messed up man. Restoration happens when we choose to humble ourselves, turn from our sinful ways, and walk with God. For God "does
not forget the cry of the afflicted" (Ps. 9:12). In the end, the messed up
man in your life may become "even greater than before."

Six Things to Do While God Works on the Proud Man

1. Don't personalize it.
2. Resist the urge to play the blame game.
3. Stay out of the whirlwind.
4. Create a safe place.
5. Hand it over to God.
6. Keep praying.

Moving Beyond the Mess

1. How would you define *pride*?
2. How would you define the men in your life (boastful, humble, gentle, balanced, appreciative, arrogant, shy, depressed, gloomy)?
3. Consider your relationship with each individual man you've characterized above. What steps have you taken to walk with that man? Who is more prideful in your relationship? Reflect on Proverbs 16:18. What is it saying?
4. Reflect on a moment when your own pride busted out in a bad way.
5. Read Proverbs 11:2. What wisdom can women take away from this Scripture passage?
6. *Moving to a healthier place:* Look back over "Six Things to Do While God Works on the Proud Man." In what areas might you have more difficulty? What steps can you take to move beyond pride-filled, messed up moments into a healthier place (either on your own or with a man in your life)?

May the Lord humble you before His throne and raise
you up with a heart ready for healing.

3

Saul

A Reckless Ruler

*Like a city that is broken into and without walls is a man
who has no control over his spirit.*
PROVERBS 25:28

TINA ❧ Okay, let's get it over, put it out there, say the words—control freak. Someone once thrust a book into my hands titled *The Control Freak*, by Dr. Les Parrott III. I snubbed my nose at the thought. Me, controlling? Humph!

However, upon flipping through the book, I found that I did have controlling tendencies. Today I understand where many of them came from. I grew up in an unstable home with a controlling father. As a child, I had no control over my life. But as I grew, I learned to control the things I could control—for better or worse. I had no idea how to successfully manage my life.

Perhaps you too are trying to control or manage your life. But God is the only one who can regulate our lives, sprinkle peace over us like a gentle snow, and drive out the tension.

In his book, Dr. Parrott identifies ten qualities of a control freak:

1. Obnoxious
2. Tenacious
3. Invasive
4. Obsessive
5. Perfectionistic
6. Critical
7. Irritable
8. Demanding
9. Rigid
10. Closed-minded[1]

Do you recognize yourself or perhaps someone you live with? Are controlling women different from controlling men? Do men exhibit controlling behaviors in a more aggressive way than women? In truth, a controlling person is really someone who's out of control. Perhaps the men in your life are reckless in trying to rule their homes.

DAVE ✵ Control seems preferable to what we typically think of as its opposite—chaos. But I want to suggest that the opposite of control is not chaos. It is *trust*, and trust is far preferable to control. We want to control because we fear the outcome of letting God be in control. We fear we won't be taken care of, won't have what we need, or will be taken advantage of. But trying to be in control is futile, because in reality there is very little that we can control.

I wouldn't consider myself a control freak, but I've had my moments. I've seen trouble coming and fought, fumed, and frazzled myself trying to control circumstances and situations. One of the most impossible things to control is something walking around on two legs called a human being. I've manipulated and thrown temper tantrums trying to get another person to behave the way that seemed best to me. After all, doesn't someone need to control the bad behaviors of others?

But after fifty-one years of life on this planet, including nearly thirty years of marriage, I've concluded that the only thing I can control is my attitude. Everything else is fantasy. I've tried to control my kids. I've tried to control my churches. I've tried to control my dog, Gavin. I've even tried to control Tina (not a good idea). A sure sign of when I'm trying to control things, people, or circumstances is that I get frustrated, develop a bad attitude, and usually end up angry.

Many biblical men struggled with control issues. One in particular stands out: Saul, the first king of Israel.

A Difficult Wait

I hope you'll take time to read chapters 9 and 10 of 1 Samuel. You will find an amazing man of God who appears to have no flaws. He is a "choice and handsome man . . . taller than any of the people" (1 Sam. 9:2). A man who is concerned for others and their feelings. He doesn't want his family to worry about him, and he wants to make sure he has the right present for the prophet Samuel when he meets him.

Saul is anointed by Samuel as ruler of Israel. We see Saul's heart changed by God and the Spirit of God coming upon him. Saul is even able to prophesy with the prophets of God. And on top of that, Saul appears humble. When the time comes for his public proclamation as king of Israel, he is found hiding. "Samuel said to all the people, 'Do you see him whom the Lord has chosen? Surely there is no one like him among all the people.' So all the people shouted and said, 'Long live the king!'" (10:24). Who wouldn't want a man like Saul as king? Who wouldn't want a man like Saul in their family? What a guy!

It's often said that if you squeeze a person, you'll find out what's really in him. Apply enough pressure and he'll show his true colors. Saul is squeezed pretty hard in 1 Samuel 13. His son Jonathan has attacked one of the Philistine garrisons and provoked the Philistine army. "The Philistines assembled to fight with Israel, 30,000 chariots and 6,000 horsemen, and people like the sand which is on the seashore in abundance. . . . When the men of Israel saw that they were in a strait (for the people were hard-pressed), then the people hid themselves in caves, in thickets, in cliffs, in cellars, and in pits" (vv. 5–6). You can almost feel the pressure building on the young king. "But as for Saul, he was still in Gilgal, and all the people followed him trembling" (v. 7). Saul is still in control of things, but just barely. The people with him are trembling—never a good sign for an army.

"Now he waited seven days, according to the appointed time set by Samuel, but Samuel did not come to Gilgal; and the people were scattering from him" (v. 8). The trembling people have become a scattering people. Imagine yourself in Saul's shoes. You can feel the pit starting to grow in your stomach. Thirty-six thousand of the enemy's chariots and horseman, and what seems like an endless infantry, are prepared for battle against you. Your troops are scared to death and starting to desert. You've waited a gut-wrenching seven days for Samuel, the prophet of God, to show up and offer the prewar sacrifice. The seventh day is ending, and still Samuel is nowhere in sight. You've got to do something!

"So Saul said, 'Bring to me the burnt offering and the peace offerings.' And *he* offered the burnt offering" (v. 9, emphasis mine).

Saul's fear of the unknown and his attempt to control what seems to be impending chaos lead him to commit a great sin. Taking matters into his own hands, he offers a sacrifice that is beyond his pay grade.

Let's put it in perspective. Saul isn't fleeing the battlefield, denying his faith, or hiding among the luggage. He is doing a lot that's right. Moreover, he faces a seemingly numberless army, his own forces have already dwindled to a paltry six hundred men, and these men don't have any swords or spears (v. 22). Saul does not trust that things are going to turn out well if nothing changes, and I wouldn't either. I too would be overwhelmed with doubt and despair, and likely pretty ticked at Samuel. Where is that guy anyway?

Here is what I know to be true: messed up men will often panic and try to control the chaos. Waiting is one of the hardest spiritual disciplines.

Waiting is spelled T-R-U-S-T.

> ## What Is TRUST?
>
> **T**otally rely on God.
>
> **R**efuse to act without God's direction.
>
> **U**nconditionally obey God's plan.
>
> **S**ubmit to God's control.
>
> **T**ake God's timing.

God wants us to trust Him and resist the urge to control. Speaking personally, when I try to control, it's because I'm worried and scared, and I want to avoid pain. I've got six hundred men with sticks taking on a well-armed enemy, and the outcome doesn't look good.

Ironically, Samuel shows up right after the sacrifice is offered and rebukes Saul for his hastiness. As a result, Saul's kingdom will not endure. He has acted foolishly, and consequences are coming.

So how does the battle turn out? Well, Saul and Jonathan and their six hundred farmers defeat the enemy. And I believe that even if Saul had waited another week for Samuel to show up, they would have won the battle. Even if all that remained were Saul and Jonathan, they would have won the battle.

The many times when I've attempted to take control have led sometimes to success and sometimes to failure. But they have been my decisions. The decisions your own messed up man makes are not yours to own, and they are not yours to control. In the same way that God wants to teach your man how to trust, God is also teaching you how to trust.

TINA ❀ You and I are not alone in our dealing with controlling men. Women in Scripture also faced strong men, as well as men who stepped outside healthy boundaries. Perhaps the man in your life likes things done a certain way; he isn't abusive, just controlling. (If you are dealing with an abusive man, seek help from a licensed professional.)

Maybe your man falls apart in out-of-control situations, and you have no idea how to respond. How do you live with such a man? How did the women in Saul's life handle living with a controlling man?

Ahinoam, the Wife

Not much is said about Ahinoam, Saul's wife. Again, in biblical times women were treated and looked upon in a different light than in today's world. There is some debate among biblical scholars as to whether David married Saul's wife or another woman also named Ahinoam. If David indeed married Saul's wife, then we have a lot to talk about.

David's army grew in strength and numbers when it came to the war between Saul and himself. He was a wise man; his tactics and maneuvers to assure his ascendancy to the throne were well-conceived. It would not surprise me if David had taken Ahinoam as his wife. But no one really knows.

So many questions about this young lady's life, and no one to answer them! However, one thing we do know about Ahinoam is her name. And that is important. From the very beginning, biblical names carried significance. From Adam, the "first man," to Moses, meaning "drawn," names had meaning and purpose.

Many of us can trace our names back generation to generation. You may live in New York City but were named after your great aunt, Bertha May. No offense to Bertha Mays, but wouldn't you prefer a name that fit you and your personality and perhaps New York?

People ask me, "Did your name come from Christina?"

"No, just Tina."

"Not Kristin, Valentina, or something like that?"

"No, just Tina."

My mother named me Tina because a premature birth left me very tiny. Someone said "Tiny Tina," and it stuck. I outgrew Tiny, but I'm still Tina.

In my younger years, my special-needs brother decided to call me

"Teener Wiener." To this day, he still calls me that. *Why?* I have no idea. I hated it and tried to correct him, but in the end, if calling me a giant frankfurter makes him happy, I'm at peace with it.

But while our own names may not make sense, biblical names were chosen to fit the person, culture, religion, and so on. They were "story names." Story names told stories and passed down history.

Ahinoam means "'brother of pleasantries' in the sense of 'pleasing or dear brother.'"[2] Based on her name, we can assume she radiated a beauty that pleased others. We can imagine a young woman whom people enjoyed being around; a woman who spoke softly and perhaps refrained from forcing her opinions on others, respectful of her husband and a delight in every way. Married to a king, she needed to demonstrate those qualities publicly, but if she also exhibited that kind of character behind the scenes, then that says something more.

Of course, I'm speculating; we don't really know Ahinoam's true character, beyond what her name implies. What was her life like, married to Saul? Did she simply follow through with her duties as a king's wife and let life fall as it might? Did she experience what some women in today's world experience from their husbands—wrath and control? For Saul clearly exhibited controlling characteristics. He could be obnoxious, invasive, irritable, demanding, rigid, and closed-minded.

Just how controlling was Saul? First Samuel chapters 13–18 reveal the following:

- Told to wait seven days for Samuel, Saul instead took matters into his own hands and made the sacrificial offering himself.
- Saul foolishly forbade his soldiers to eat any food before going into battle.
- Saul ordered the death of his own son for disobeying an order.
- Ignoring God's command to utterly destroy the Amelekites and everything they owned, Saul spared their king, Agag, as well as their sheep and goats.
- Saul turned against David and spent the rest of his days trying to murder him.

How did Saul's women respond? How did Ahinoam keep the integrity of her name—or did she? If in the middle of Saul's abusive and controlling behavior she somehow maintained her character and personality, then she is quite the woman. Did people see her in the center of Saul's messed up life and say, "That is Ahinoam, the Pleasant One." We'd like to think so, because we admire women like that.

A name says so much. What is *my* name, I wonder? What do people call me? Yikes! I'm a little scared to hear the answer. What about the woman living with a controlling man? What character does she display? What do people call her? You see, a man's controlling behavior can change a woman—change the name others give her—the name she gives herself.

Rizpah, the Concubine

Of all the women in the Bible, Saul's concubine, Rizpah, is one of the most determined mothers a child could have. She is also a mother who suffered great loss because of the man in her life.

I step into her shoes and immediately weep. What misery she endured! The magnitude of her bravery, strength, and affection dwarf my moments of strength.

Rizpah could not control Saul and his mood swings. She could not control his behavior, his jealousy, or his treatment of others. And she could not control his enemies who, out of revenge, would one day require the death of her sons because of Saul's sin.

After Saul's death when David took the throne, Israel sat in drought for three years. After seeking the Lord, David learned the drought was due to Saul's execution of the Gibeonites. David asked the Gibeonites what he could do to make things right. Their reply: hand over seven of Saul's grandsons to be hanged (2 Sam. 21:1–6).

Though David spared Jonathan's son, Mephibosheth (v. 7), he surrendered Rizpah's two sons along with five of Saul's grandchildren. Afterward, Rizpah went out to where the seven men were hanging, spread a piece of sackcloth over a rock, and camped out on it. Over time, the stench from the bodies attracted buzzards, but Rizpah threw stones, swatted at the birds with long limbs, and yelled at them, "Get away! Leave my sons alone!" Every sound caught her attention. Day after day, night after night, she stood vigil over the blackened, decaying bodies—unable to control the outcome of what unfolded, but managing what she could.

Manage or Mayhem

A few months ago I saw a strange bird standing out in the back yard. Every time I walked outside, the bird squealed and squawked, creating a huge ruckus. I thought it rather strange, exhibiting this behavior while standing in an open field. Over time my son and I realized the bird had made a nest on the ground and laid four eggs. Day after day we watched the mother and father switch off in caring for their babies. Neither rain, heat, nor flooding kept them from their watch. Wild emotions encased my heart. Somehow I found myself sucked into their life—responsible for making sure the eggs were safe. I only had one concern—our one-hundred-pound lab. Each time Gavin roamed near the nest, we scolded, "No!" We did our best to hide and protect the eggs. We even surrounded the nest with rocks to make sure we didn't accidently step on them.

Early one morning I let Gavin out to relieve himself, carefully watching to make sure he did not go near the nest. All was well until Gavin's ears raised and head turned. He took off like a bolt of lightning and dug his big nose into the nest. I ran to the door and yelled, "Gavin, no!" My heart raced. I stepped one foot out the door and looked down at my nighty and our chain-link fence. I ran fast and grabbed what I could. Suddenly I found myself running across the soaked yard, barefoot and all, wearing my father's plaid flannel robe and swinging a large blue umbrella. I'm sure I woke the neighbors. One look at me and no doubt glaring eyes found me completely mad! Sadly, Gavin ate the birds before I reached him. My heart sank. *How could this happen? And on my watch?* After putting the dog in the doghouse, I cried for hours. Why? Because I couldn't save the birds. As hours passed, I came to understand that I never had control over something I felt I *did* have control over. Such a difficult reminder. And our souls ache and empathize with Rizpah in her desperation to control an outcome brought on by the man in her life.

Rizpah could not rescue Saul from his controlling behavior, his enemies, or the impact his mistakes had on her life. Instead, Rizpah managed what she *could* and left the rest up to God.

Here is what Rizpah managed:

+ The way she responded to the outcome of Saul's sin
+ What she did with her time after the deaths of her sons
+ How she would protect her sons' bodies from animals and birds
+ Her method of ensuring her sons got a proper burial, no matter how long it took
+ Her commitment to see her task through to the end

Rizpah probably prayed for the rains to fall and end the three-year drought. Maybe she hoped David would see her actions and have mercy upon her and her family. In the end, King David gave her sons and Saul's grandchildren a proper burial.

Unlike Rizpah's courageous display, some women may have hidden from it all. Are you hiding from a controlling man or your inability to control your circumstances? If I were there, I would fall to my knees, stretch out my hand beneath the bed, and encourage you to come out. I would want you to hear the words of Isaiah—how God desires to "encourage the exhausted, and strengthen the feeble." I would say to your anxious heart, "Take courage, fear not. Behold, your God will come with vengeance. . . . He will save you" (Isa. 35:3–4). God will save you. But you must move out from beneath the bed, away from the corner, out of the darkness. Step away from hurt into healing and a better place. My heart wanted to scoop up the bird's nest and set it in a safe place, but because the mother built it as she did I could not help her. You have a choice, my friend—to either stay where you are or move out

of the darkness toward healing. Part of Rizpah's healing came in her
determination to see a proper burial.

So while God is working on your messed up man, there are things in
life you *can* manage:

+ Whether or not you will remain a victim
+ Whom you will allow to speak into your life
+ How you respond to what you perceive as messed up, controlling
  moments
+ How you trust God to bring you through each day
+ How you trust God to change the man in your life—and yourself
+ Whether to make a change if you're in physical danger

Once you determine that you're sick of being sick and tired, you want
a better you, and you're ready to find healing, set healthy boundaries,
work on communication, and start living your life, then you aren't as
controlled as you may feel. Here are five things to practice when living
with a controlling man:

1. *Make a decision to change.* Assess your situation. Conclude that
   your messed up man's controlling behavior has affected you. Has
   the controlling behavior belittled, trapped, confined, beaten you
   down, hurt, wounded, or stifled you? If so, then admit you've been
   hurt and you want to do something about it. Make a decision to
   work through your hurt. God corrects attitudes and hands out
   new hearts.

   Ezekiel 36:26 says, "I will give you a new heart and put a new
   spirit in you" (NIV). Decide that even in trouble, you'll turn your
   hurts over to God and allow Him to heal and direct you. That
   means getting to a safe place if the controlling man hurts you.

2. *Rebuild.* If you feel beaten down, then it's time to rebuild. God has
   an incredible way of fixing broken pieces. Start by allowing Him

to rebuild your confidence. Hebrews 10:35–36 says, "Therefore, do not throw away your confidence, which has a great reward. For you have need of endurance, so that when you have done the will of God, you may receive what was promised." Confidence instills endurance and endurance helps us move toward healing. Talk to your pastor, get into counseling, or work through Christian self-help books. Begin to see yourself as God sees you: as a precious daughter of Christ.

3. *Shift your thinking.* I recently heard a pastor say, "A renewed mind lives from a place of wholeness, not brokenness." God is the only one who can bring our broken thoughts back into alignment with His—transforming the view of ourselves. Your worth depends upon what God says about you, not the opinions of others. Build your self-respect. By doing so, you will find the courage to get help in setting healthy boundaries and finding your voice. Replace negative thoughts with good ones. Replace "I'm worthless" with "I am fearfully and wonderfully made; wonderful are Your works, and my soul knows it very well" (Ps. 139:14). Replace "I can't do anything right" with "I can do all things through Him who strengthens me" (Phil. 4:13). Accept that "we all stumble in many ways" (James 3:2), and it's okay.

   Replace the lies that come from Satan's mouth with God's words and perspective on who you are. "The enemy is empowered by human agreement. To agree with anything he says gives him a place to kill, steal, and destroy. We fuel the cloud of oppression by agreeing with our enemy."[3] We do not have to hold on to words that hurt and steal our value—nor accept them as truth.

4. *Surround yourself with positive people.* People who have nothing good to say about others will eventually bring you down.

5. *Value yourself—because the Lord does.* He formed you, created you, ordained your steps, and gave His life so you may live. He will rescue you if you let Him.

I love the story of Queen Vashti in the book of Esther. After seven days of partying, Vashti's drunken husband, King Ahasuerus of Persia, commanded that she be fetched and displayed, crown in hand, before all his guests. Despite the harsh consequences she would surely face for disobeying the king, Queen Vashti determined that valuing herself was far more important than anything else.

The Right Ending

Saul lost his throne, kingdom, family, and life. I wish all relationships had a fairy-tale ending, but life is much harder than that. Women grasp at whatever they can control in their relationships to get the right ending.

In my younger years, I used to fish with my dad. Deep in the woods, at his secret fishing hole, we often caught small perch. Emotions heightened with each nibble. Reeling in, we often found a fish at the end of the line, but other times the hook was bare, stripped of the bait. When we did catch a fish, often we released it back into the pond.

As women, we spend much of our lives catching and releasing. Remember the day you caught your man (or he caught you)? My own man walked into my life wearing a red-and-white baseball T-shirt with half-sleeves and a baseball cap. He sported a mullet (it was the 80s), and his dark hair hung out the back of his cap. His smile knocked me off my feet. Wow! Even today, that memory ignites sparks. Did I catch him, or he me? I think we caught each other.

Catching is easy; releasing is the hard part. But the only control we really have with our men is the ability to release them. I don't know what letting go of a controlling man will look like for you. I do know that if we can release our hurts, fears, and concerns to God, He knows how to take care of them—and the messed up man. It's up to you, my friend. Will you maintain your grip on your catch, or will you release him to God?

Release doesn't mean quitting your relationship; it means surrendering your relationship. When we surrender something, we relinquish control over it. Ironically, we release our control of the controlling person.

One author puts it this way: "Surrender means giving up, as opposed to giving in. Through surrender, there comes a genuine relinquishing of our rights to Jesus Christ as the Lord of our lives."[4]

Our freedom comes when we set others free. So what does release look like?

+ Letting go of trying to control the messed up men in our life
+ Letting go of trying to control our own life
+ Loving ourselves enough to set healthy boundaries
+ Seeking help when we need it

Jennifer Strickland, a former supermodel who helps women build a healthy self-image, said, "When you are young, you do not realize what the world can do to a boy, or what a boy can do to himself. I could not fix the problem [boys] had with substance abuse, depression, school, money, and more. Although I tried to throw a rope, they had neither the hope nor the faith to grab it, and I certainly had no muscle to raise them."[5]

Boys grow up and become men. How many ropes have we thrown them? We cannot fix the messed up men in our life, nor do we, as Jennifer says, have the muscle to raise them from their messes. We can only pray they find the hope and faith to grab hold of the rope God throws out to them.

If the messed up man allows God to capture his heart, then God will do a great work in his life. God will release him from his sins and renew a right spirit within him. Praise God for outcomes like that. They're the right ending, the ending we want, desire, and pray for. May it be so, my friends.

Well, what happened to the momma bird? After telling my son about Gavin's mess up, he said, "She's probably off making a new nest now." "Probably true son, probably true."

Five Things to Practice When Living with a Controlling Man

1. Begin to **change** your attitude and circumstances by setting your thoughts on Christ.
2. **Rebuild** your self-esteem and confidence.
3. **Shift** negative thoughts into positive ones.
4. **Surround** yourself with encouraging people.
5. **Value** yourself as God values you. Allow Him to rescue you.

Moving Beyond the Mess

1. How would you define control? Time to confess—are you a control freak?
2. Do you now, or have you ever, lived with a controlling person? How did you cope? Perhaps you're the controller in the relationship. How would the man in your life cope with you?
3. What are your thoughts on why Saul chose to make the sacrifice rather than wait on Samuel the prophet? What drives men to control?
4. How do you suppose having a controlling husband impacted the women in Saul's life? How can a controlling husband impact a woman?
5. Talk about women today who live with controlling men. How have the ways men control women today changed from in the past?
6. *Moving to a healthier place:* Read Galatians 5:22–23. The fruit of the Spirit involves what kind of control? Controlling people lack

it. What are ways in which a woman can bring self-control into
her relationship with a controlling man?

———————

*May God bring peace and light into your life. With
each breath may you exhale stress, tension, and anxiety,
understanding that through Christ, healing takes place.*

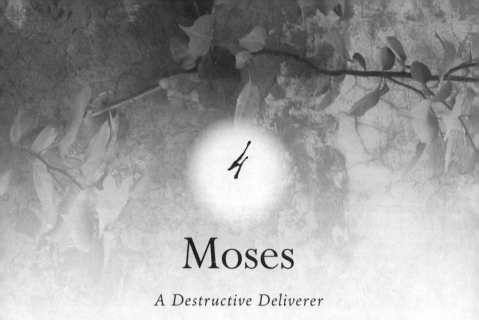

4

Moses

A Destructive Deliverer

> *If an angry man raises the dead, God is still*
> *displeased with his anger.*
>
> Agatho, fourth-century Egyptian monk

TINA ❀ When I was a teenager, a woman from my church once asked me to help make salad by cutting a tomato. My heart raced as I held the knife. *How do I cut it?* It wasn't that I didn't know how; my mother taught me how to do things in the kitchen. My hesitancy was rooted in something my father had planted in my heart—fear. What if I cut the tomato wrong?

Finally I asked, "How do I cut it?"

The woman looked at me and smiled. "Any way you want."

Even then I didn't know where to start. It's strange how something so simple can become a huge obstacle, but that's the impact another person's anger can have. There was a time when I couldn't put a stamp on an envelope without making sure it was straight, and to this day, when my husband gets agitated over politics or football, anxiety stirs inside me.

Neil Anderson and Rich Miller wrote:

> We have all developed one or more flesh patterns, or strong-holds, of anger. We may be aware of what our patterns are, and we may be finding great success in overcoming those aspects of the flesh through the liberating power of the Spirit. On the other hand, we may not be aware of our own flesh patterns and therefore have done little to overcome them. Many people in this condition just assume that this is the way they are—and others are just going to have to live with it as they have learned to live with it. Or we may be somewhere in the middle— uncomfortable with how we manage our anger, but lacking the insight to do anything about it.[1]

I justified my father's anger by telling myself, "He's not a believer." But believers struggle with anger too. The wisest and most scholarly struggle as well. Even those called "friend of God" struggle with anger. And the messed up man? He certainly struggles.

DAVE ❧ Moses—what an amazing man! The highs and lows of his life are breathtaking. He is rescued from certain death as a Hebrew infant and raised in the household of Egyptian royalty. But when power gives way to murder, Moses loses his position and flees to the back side of the desert. Restored and recalled by God, he returns to Egypt with nothing but a staff and a divine calling to liberate what some believe to be more than a million Hebrew slaves. Then, wandering in the desert with the children of Israel, Moses creates a nation, builds an army, and changes history. No doubt, Moses was a mighty man of God!

Yet, like your messed up man, Moses had issues to overcome. For

Moses was an angry man, and his anger would create some devastating consequences in his life.

"Now it came about in those days, when Moses had grown up, that he went out to his brethren and looked on their hard labors; and he saw an Egyptian beating a Hebrew, one of his brethren. So he looked this way and that, and when he saw there was no one around, he struck down the Egyptian and hid him in the sand" (Exod. 2:11–12).

Moses was either very arrogant, very foolish, or very angry. Didn't he know he would get caught? There was a witness to his crime—the same Hebrew slave he had saved from the Egyptian's brutality. By the next day, "Moses was afraid and said, 'Surely the matter has become known'" (Exod. 2:14).

Moses committed a crime of passion. He wasn't thinking about consequences, nor was he interested in using his position in Pharaoh's house to restrain the abusive overseer. He simply wanted the man dead.

I've never killed anyone, but I know what it's like to be out-of-control angry. In times past, I sometimes had to watch myself closely. A few criticisms added to my simmering insecurity could escalate me to the boiling point. Almost without warning, I would spew defensive justifications and pointed jabs. Perhaps, like me and many men, Moses reacted to an external stimulus that collided with his feelings of shame, guilt, unworthiness, etc. Who knows? What we do know is that he killed a man, and then, within twenty-four hours, he began to experience the full effect of his rash action. Packing his bag in a hurry, he started out across the desert, where he would spend the next forty years of his life.

Between a Rock and a Hard Place

Moses's life offers many opportunities for us to speculate about the strengths and weaknesses of his temperament. Let's consider another incident that was as critical to his future as his killing of the Egyptian.

Numbers 20 describes how the people assembled against Moses because there was no water to drink. This was serious stuff, and Moses and Aaron did the right thing by going before the Lord and seeking his counsel. God's response was crystal-clear: "Take the rod; and you and your brother Aaron assemble the congregation and speak to the rock before their eyes, that it may yield its water" (Num. 20:8). Now notice Moses's response to God's direction: "So Moses took the rod from before the Lord, just as He had commanded him; and Moses and Aaron gathered the assembly before the rock. And he said to them, 'Listen now, you rebels; shall we bring forth water for you out of this rock?' Then Moses lifted up his hand and struck the rock twice with his rod" (Num. 20:9–11).

It's baffling why Moses would deviate from the Lord's clear command. God had already done so much on Israel's behalf, and Moses surely trusted that God could and would deliver His people again. The text doesn't mention Moses's anger, but his insults to the people reveal an angry man.

Even so, abundant water flowed from the rock in response to Moses's actions. But God didn't overlook Moses's behavior. "The Lord said to Moses and Aaron, 'Because you have not believed Me, to treat Me as holy in the sight of the sons of Israel, therefore you shall not bring this assembly into the land which I have given them'" (Num. 20:12).

There it is. Moses's disobedience was going to cost him a great deal. Because of his anger, he would be deprived of the very thing his entire life had been pointing toward—the ultimate deliverance of the people into their homeland.

Notice the root of Moses's sin: "Because you have not believed Me, to treat Me as holy . . ." (Num. 20:12). This is huge. It is the root not just of anger but of all sin: unbelief. We see it transparently in our own anger. Things don't go our way. People don't do what we think is best. We grow frustrated and annoyed. We get angry. Rather than trusting God to work all things for our benefit, we intervene.

Instead of speaking to the rock, Moses yelled at the people and struck the rock; instead of trusting God, we ourselves manipulate people and strike out at whatever stands in our way. The consequences are devastating for us, our families, and everyone around us. As with Moses, our actions well may cost us our life's goals.

Perhaps your messed up man finds himself, like Moses, between a rock and a hard place. Like Moses, he responds with anger. And you have no idea what to do with that angry man in your life. Perhaps you need to start by coming to the place the psalmist arrived at:

> For who is God besides the LORD? And who is the Rock except our God? (Ps. 18:31 NIV)

> For in the day of trouble he will keep me safe in his dwelling; he will hide me in the shelter of his sacred tent and set me high upon a rock. (Ps. 27:5 NIV)

God the Rock picks us up and sets us down on a big boulder, beyond the chaos of the rushing water. He sneaks us through the flap of His sacred tent to keep us safe. The hard part is allowing God to pick us up. Do we go willingly, or do we kick and scream through the process? Do we search for Him, run to Him? Let us come to the place where He truly becomes *the Rock* in our lives.

In the process, as you deal with angry men in your life, remember and practice this acronym: RELAX.

> **R**emain calm. It takes two to have an argument. That said, you can prevent arguments by learning to remain calm, breathing evenly, and refusing to add any emotional heat to whatever may already be happening.

> **E**mpathize. Try to understand where someone is coming from. Empathy looks beyond the words and actions and seeks to understand the source of an issue. It feels the other person's pain and relates from the heart to his hurt, frustration, and way of thinking, even if it's wrong thinking. Empathy does not mean overlooking, dismissing, or justifying bad attitudes or behavior; it means understanding the other person.

Listen. We would all do well to learn to hear what is really being said—and what is *not* being said. Words often get twisted and meanings misunderstood. An aggressive attack might mean unfair accusations, belittling comments, and storming complaints. Get in the habit of repeating back to the person what you heard him say and then asking, "Did I hear that right?"

Act to uphold your boundaries. We all need to set and maintain healthy ones. If someone violates your space, sanity, or safety, then remove yourself from the situation. Say something like, "We can try to discuss this later when our emotions are not quite so raw."

X-amine your role. A good friend, Tom Pals, taught me, "Just because it's personal doesn't mean you have to take it personally." Other people's issues can easily overflow into our space, and we take their words and actions personally. Often we can defuse situations when we simply step back and realize that someone's anger or bad attitude really has nothing to do with us. Let the other person throw his temper tantrum without you. (However, if you do play a part in the situation, then own up to it and accept responsibility.)

Five Ways to Relax When Dealing with an Angry Man
Remain calm
Empathize
Listen
Act to uphold your boundaries
X-amine your role

A Good Need

TINA ❦ Sixteen-year-old Megan[2] parked the car and eased out of it. All-too-familiar sounds were coming from the house. *He's angry again.* She ascended the rickety steps and opened the door, and a heaviness grabbed her throat as she stepped inside.

Then it came—the *thwack!* of a hand hitting another person. It was a sound Megan had become accustomed to, yet loathed. As often as she had heard it, it never lost its impact on her vulnerable heart.

She paused momentarily. *Just get past them,* she thought, but long-suppressed emotions rose inside her, grabbing at her gut, pounding to get out, and fury awakened and surged through her. *No! This time will be different.* This time she wouldn't just slide by; pretend nothing is happening. She let her anger carry her across the room, and suddenly there she was, standing directly in front of her father, her trembling finger pointing right in his face. "Keep your hands to yourself! Don't ever hit her again!" she bellowed.

Megan shuddered in the wake of her own wrath. She had never raised her voice to her father, and now the churning in her stomach forced its way to the top. She raced to the bathroom. Her mother entered shortly after and placed a cold cloth on Megan's flushed face. "It's all right now," her mom said. "It's all right."

Do you identify with Megan's story? Megan's mother wasn't the only one who felt the impact of her husband's actions; Megan did as well. Perhaps you grew up with an angry, abusive man. Or maybe you live with a messed up man who struggles with anger. And at some point, his anger ignited a reciprocal anger in you. Growing up in that kind of environment makes it difficult to find your voice. And when you do find it, you may not know how to use it appropriately and effectively.

When my father drank, he was an angry man. His unpredictable behavior scared me. One minute he appeared fine, but the next he could explode like a volcano. I had no idea how my dad's anger impacted me until I left for college. That's when I discovered that I myself had become an angry person, so angry at my father's anger that I couldn't see I was behaving just as badly—until one life-changing weekend.

It started with a conversation with my dad and brother on the pay-phone (this was before cell phones took over). Anger burned deep; I got so mad I thought I might burst. I'm sure the entire neighborhood heard me.

That Sunday at church, a morning I'll never forget, the pastor spoke on forgiveness. I still fumed; bitterness and anger formed a callus over my soul. But carrying the weight of my emotions was exhausting.

At the close of his message, the pastor asked, "Will you turn your bitterness over to God? Will you allow yourself to forgive others who have hurt you?" I was safe and out of the home now, yet I wanted to stand up and shout, "No!" But something else happened. Two simple words arrested my anger: *Will you?*

"I want to, Lord," I whispered. "I need to. Help me. Please forgive me."

The only way to describe what happened next is to have you envision a whirlwind—not a tornado but a gentle swirl of wind. The top of it touched my head and ran down my entire body. I felt cocooned by this strange sensation. I shivered and tingled all over. It ran down my body and up again. When the wind stopped, tears ran down my cheeks, and I felt a freedom I hadn't felt in a long while. The heaviness was gone, the burden lifted, and I felt unleashed. I found myself looking at a huge chalkboard on which I had written every hurt, disappointment, fear, unfairness, and angry moment I ever experienced with my dad. Some-how the chalkboard had been wiped clean. There it was, but I had no idea what had been written on it before that moment.

I wish our freedom could always come at the snap of a finger or mag-ically appear in a fresh breeze, but it rarely happens that way. Usually we have to do the hard work to get there. I understand now that a mir-acle took place in my life. God is the burden crusher and the freedom fighter. He has the power to change lives. However, I've concluded that a few things needed to take place in my heart in order for God to do His work:

I needed to be tired of my anger. I was weary of feeling burdened and angry all the time. Constantly bearing the weight of my painful emotions took tremendous effort, and I felt exhausted, in mind, body, and soul.

I needed to be ready. I came to a point when the opportunity to wave a white flag stared me in the face, and I took it. Surrender. I needed it. I willingly handed my suffering over to God.

God will allow us to carry our burdens around with us the rest of our lives if we want to. But I have enough weight I'm carrying around. Do I really need that as well? God is always whispering, "Come to Me, all who are weary and heavy-laden, and I will give you rest. Take My yoke upon you and learn from Me, for I am gentle and humble in heart, and YOU WILL FIND REST FOR YOUR SOULS. For My yoke is easy and My burden is light" (Matt. 11:28–30).

I needed to be touched. The Holy Spirit came and touched me. I never expected it, and as a young college student I was amazed at how quickly the Lord's touch turned my heart around. But I also asked God to come and help me. I requested His presence.

The freedom God brought to me allowed me to come face to face with a man who hurt me and love him anyway. Many years later, my dad gave his life to Christ, stopped drinking, and changed. Even now I reflect on moments of him fixing broken-down cars, rising early to make breakfast, driving hours for a visit, and sneaking vanilla ice-cream cones. The father-daughter relationship I longed for blossomed into something very special.

How do you find freedom from your own anger and unforgiveness? Start by recognizing how tired you are of your situation. Get sick of it. Release your burdens. Invite God to change your life.

How to Live with an Angry, Messed Up Man

Several biblical women give great examples of dos and don'ts when living with a messed up man battling anger. I share their entire stories in the book I coauthored with Dena Dyer, *Wounded Women of the Bible*, and I would like to highlight some helpful insights here.

Ichabod's mother (1 Sam. 4:8–21)

The mother of Ichabod was married to a corrupt priest who openly committed adultery. He stole offerings from the Israelites, disrespected his father, and paid no attention to God's leadership and direction. He took the ark of the covenant into battle, only to have it stolen by the enemy.

> **Don't**—turn bitter. When Ichabod's mother heard that her husband, brother-in-law, and father-in-law had died and the ark was captured, she turned bitter. She believed that in her circumstance, the glory of the Lord had departed. Her bitterness caused her to name her newborn son "Ichabod," meaning "no glory."

> **Do**—hold on. Thessalonians tells us to "hold on to what is good, reject every kind of evil" (1 Thess. 5:21–22 niv). Ichabod's mother lost sight of what was good: her son—a son who could take a different path than his father and bring honor to his family name. Though she died shortly after giving birth, she could have blessed her newborn and named him *Kabowd*, which means "glory!"

Before my father changed, my mother faced devastation every day of her life. I often wondered where she got her strength to endure my father's fury. She prayed, read her Bible, focused on the Lord, remained steadfastly by God's side, and determined that, in the end, God would have the glory. And He did!

The anger in a man is a symptom of something deeper. We see the outward flesh and sin. God sees them too, but He also sees beyond them to the good in the man He created. If I hadn't seen it with my own eyes, I would never have believed it possible—that God could turn a wrath-filled man into a peace-filled son.

Jezebel (1 Kings 21)

King Ahab and his queen, Jezebel, were evil people who fed off each other's sinful behavior. Finding Ahab depressed over another man's refusal to sell him the family vineyard, Jezebel had the man stoned to death so Ahab could obtain the property. While Jezebel was responsible for her own actions, she fed off her husband's unhealthy behavior. It's not so different from what happens in relationships today.

Consider this profound statement in the biblical account: "There was never anyone like Ahab, who sold himself to do evil in the eyes of the Lord, urged on by Jezebel his wife" (v. 25 NIV).

Wow! I would never want to hear the reverse said about me: that I did evil in the eyes of the Lord because I was influenced by my husband. If the man in your life gets angry, recognize that his emotions belong to him. You don't have to own them or rise up in the same way. Through Christ, who gives you strength, you can change the way you've always reacted to his anger.

Don't—feed off your man's behavior. Something happens to us when faced with another person's anger. We often turn inward or allow our own anger to boil upward. Before we know it, we're screaming at the person who made us mad. We see from Ahab and Jezebel's relationship that they fed off each other's negative behavior.

Do—plant God's Word in your heart. Listen to James: "Understand this, my dear brothers and sisters: You must all be quick to listen, slow to speak, and slow to get angry. Human anger does not produce the righteousness God desires. So get rid of all the filth and evil in your lives, and humbly accept the word God has planted in your hearts, for it has the power to save your souls" (James 1:19–21 NLT). Let us fill our hearts with God's Word, so that what comes out of our mouths can be more of God than of our flesh.

We all struggle. Even when writing this chapter, my husband and I began a discussion, that turned into a disagreement, that turned into . . . well, you know. We weren't quick that day in God's ways, and we weren't slow either. "Quick to listen"—nope, didn't get there. "Slow to speak"— nope, not there either. "Slow to get angry"—strike three, and we parted ways like the Red Sea. I like that we always come back together to sort through those moments. The only way we can do that is to remind ourselves of what God's Word teaches, and cultivate the fruits of the Spirit that help us live in a Christlike manner with one another.

Abigail (1 Sam. 25:2–38)

Abigail lived with an unkind and foolish man. Known for his meanness, Nabal made a mess of things by getting angry at David's men and denying them food and water. A few aspects of Abigail's character, which she demonstrated in response, might help us when living with such a man.

> **Don't**—enable his behavior. Nabal's behavior was his, as were its consequences. We empower the messed up man in our life to keep doing what he does when we clean up his messes, make excuses for him, rush in to fix things, and otherwise try to keep him from reaping the fruit of his actions.

> **Do**—protect. Abigail did what she could to protect her servants and household. Without telling her husband, she gathered food and supplies for David and his men and rushed to meet them before they reached her house. You could say that Abigail rushed in to clean up Nabal's mess, but she did so for good reason—to protect innocent family members from consequences that belonged to her husband only. Her bravery and quick thinking saved lives.

> **Don't**—provoke. Later in life I learned that anger is just hurt turned inward. Before that revelation, I let my anger provoke

others. I didn't understand that I just wanted others to hurt as much as they hurt me. Now when I recognize I'm angry, I understand I'm just hurting. I look for healthy ways to work through my hurt (and sometimes I still get it wrong).

Abigail did not provoke her husband. She was careful to choose an appropriate time to talk to him.

Do—pick your moments. Abigail chose not to confront her husband during his most exposed moment. Though she could have stormed in the room and shouted, "Do you know what I just did for you!" she chose to wait. "When Abigail went to Nabal, he was in the house holding a banquet like that of a king. He was in high spirits and very drunk. So she told him nothing at all until daybreak" (1 Sam. 25:36 NIV). Abigail understood her husband and how to time a conversation that could bring fruit instead of friction.

Tamar (2 Sam. 13:1–20)

We will look at Tamar's horrific story of being raped by her own brother, Amnon, in chapter 8. For now, let me briefly share some advice from Tamar's experience, including what she did right.

Don't—remain in danger. For those who have suffered the brunt of physical abuse, my heart aches for you. I lived with that kind of anger for many years and know the devastation it can cause in another human being.

Tamar experienced the horrific wound of being raped by someone close to her, and what followed only deepened the wound. "Then Amnon hated her with intense hatred. In fact, he hated her more than he had loved her. Amnon said to her, 'Get up and get out!'" (2 Sam. 13:15 NIV).

If you live in a physically or sexually abusive situation, hope and help are available, but you must be willing to step into them. Please keep yourself and your family safe by getting out of a dangerous setting. Reach out to someone who can help you, and value yourself enough to accept that help.

Do—find a safe place. I've spoken with women who leave and then go back to their abusers time and again. It is a cycle difficult to break. But what did Tamar do? After her rape, she left the palace and went to live with her brother Absalom. Tamar found a safe place.

If you are experiencing physical abuse, please seek help. Distancing yourself doesn't mean forever. If the angry man in your life is willing to seek help, God is waiting to restore your relationship. In the end, the relationship will be better than before.

Dos and Don'ts of Living with an Angry Man	
Do	**Don't**
Hold on to hope	Turn bitter
Plant God's Word in your heart	Feed off his behavior
Protect	Enable his behavior
Pick your moments	Provoke
Find a safe place	Remain in danger

The Promised Land

"Will I make it to the Promised Land?" Maybe those aren't the words you'd use, but chances are they express the question you've been asking. What is the Promised Land? For many, the Promised Land is a home where verbal abuse no longer controls, where rage is booted out and peace is ushered in, where one walks on rose petals instead of eggshells, and where hands embrace rather than push away. In the

Promised Land, food and drink stay on tables, never splatter against walls. Hearts flutter instead of pound, and breathing is easy, not suffocating. Women put on blush to enhance their beauty, not cover their bruises.

For Moses, the Promised Land was a place abounding in fertile fields, a beautiful home for the Israelites. But it became the great prize he forfeited when he struck the rock. Moses's anger cost him the Promised Land. Will the anger in your man's life cost him? Perhaps. But we cannot fix the messed up men in our lives. Only God can do that.

What we *can* do is continue to seek the Rock, stand on the Rock, and find shelter beneath the Rock. My dear sisters, let us not forget what God told Moses to share with His people who had been held captive for so many years: "I have watched over you and have seen what has been done to you.... And I have promised to bring you up out of your misery . . . into . . . a land flowing with milk and honey" (Exod. 3:16–17 NIV).

God wants to touch you and your circumstances and instill what is lovely and good. He desires to restore your heart and home, filling even the darkest cracks with light. Let us hold on to the hope and healing that, through Christ, things can change.

Moving Beyond the Mess

1. How would you define anger?
2. Would you have considered Moses an angry man? Why do some men struggle with anger, and how is Moses similar to other men who get angry?
3. Moses became angry over various things: other people's actions (Exod. 16:20); people who didn't follow instructions or made mistakes (Lev. 10:16–17); rebellion (Num. 16:14–16). Moses was also physical with his anger (Exod. 32:19), and he expressed selfish conduct and attitudes (Num. 11:9–15; 20:10–12). Do you recognize his behavior in someone in your life? If you're discussing these questions with a group and it feels safe to share, then do so.

4. What did you like, or not like, about the actions of the women described in this chapter?
5. How can women come alongside other women who live with angry or abusive men? What are practical ways we can encourage, embrace, empathize, protect, and more? How might we become proactive in helping women rather than dismissing their hurt?
6. *Moving to a healthier place:* The following Scriptures offer smart, practical advice for managing anger, whether another person's or your own: Psalm 37:7–9; Proverbs 22:24–25; James 1:19–20. Read through each passage, consider its implications for your life, and put them into practice.

May the Lord protect you and stand in the way of an angry man. May God bring such a man to his knees and give strength to weary hearts.

Job

A Sick Soul

Suffering has been stronger than all other teaching,
and has taught me to understand what your heart used to
be. I have been bent and broken, but—I hope—
into a better shape.
CHARLES DICKENS, GREAT EXPECTATIONS

TINA 🜲 The man tears at his robe, shaves his head, and falls to the ground. Of all possible responses to the sorrows that have so relentlessly assaulted him, why this? He could scream, fight, or shake an angry fist at the heavens. Instead, he does something unexpected. He worships. The words flow from his lips: "Blessed be the name of the Lord."

In his most desperate moment, in the midst of unfathomable physical and emotional agony, Job praises God.

Women in today's world face caring for sick men—men with chronic illnesses; men who once lived vibrant lives without limitations but now face restrictions. How do women live with such men without feeling overwhelmed, discouraged, or broken? How do we follow Job's example and worship?

I once had a crush on Superman. Well, maybe the person who played Superman. I'm of the old school and looked upon Christopher Reeves as someone who could do anything. His dashing smile and demeanor melted my heart into mush. "I want to grow up and marry a man like that," I said.

Years later, my heart sank with countlesss when Superman fell from his horse. In one instant, as with Job, Superman's life changed. Christopher Reeves lived out the rest of his days with physical limitations that required others to care for his needs. It's a tragic story, yet it's one many men face: having a healthy life one minute and challenges the next.

DAVE In Job 1:1–5, we get a good feel for Job's character and ways. From the very first verse, we're told he was "blameless, upright, fearing God and turning away from evil." He habitually consecrated his children, "rising up early in the morning and offering burnt offerings according to the number of them all; for Job said, 'Perhaps my sons have sinned and cursed God in their hearts.' Thus Job did continually." What a man! Mrs. Job certainly picked a fine one. In addition, Job oozed wealth: 7,000 sheep, 3,000 camels, 1,000 oxen, 500 female donkeys, and a great many servants. Job was "the greatest of all the men of the east." Apparently he had picked the right numbers in life's lottery, because he had it made.

Job was a good enough man that one would have a difficult time suggesting his suffering was somehow his fault. In fact, Scripture tells us Job's suffering was the result of a challenge Satan addressed to God. Satan believed Job would wilt under the pressure and would ultimately curse God. God accepted the challenge, and the testing of Job's character began at once. Very quickly, Job lost his possessions, his family, and even his health. He went from riches to rags in a matter of days.

Pain and Suffering

Pain and suffering are difficult to understand. Why does a loving God allow seemingly innocent human beings to suffer? Oh, we get that suffering is an expected consequence of poor decisions. We understand the "wages of sin" stuff. What we don't get is why *good* people suffer. Why do we go through tough times when we really are trying to trust and obey God?

Jerry Bridges wrote a great book on the subject of suffering, *Trusting God Even When Life Hurts*. As a young youth pastor, I absorbed three truths from his book:

1. God is sovereign. He can do anything and everything. He can remove my pain with just a thought.
2. God is wise. He knows what He is doing and never says, "Oops!"
3. God is love. He is always looking out for my best interests.[1]

My duty, especially during trials, is to trust these three truths and pass them along to my fellow sufferers who happen to share the path of struggle with me. My belief is that suffering is somehow good for us. Pain molds and makes us into all God destined us to be.

I've had many experiences with pain, and yet to this day, my most painful physical injury dates back to the fourth grade. One afternoon after school, I found myself in the unfortunate position of being the target of a "dogpile." No fewer than six boys threw me to the ground and piled on. Believe me, it wasn't in good fun. At one point I heard something snap and instantly felt excruciating pain in my left shoulder. My collarbone had broken. At the emergency room, the doctor informed my dad that the way to heal the break was to pull my shoulders back while placing me in a brace. The doc and my dad stood behind me with both hands supporting my upper back between the shoulder blades. The doctor then proceeded to pull my shoulders back and secure the brace. I almost passed out. I've never felt such intense pain.

At the time, both the doctor and my dad seemed cruel. After all, I had done nothing to deserve such punishment. How could two grown men do something so hurtful to a small fourth grader? The truth, of course, is that the pain was unavoidable for proper healing. My shoulder is strong today (though it still aches when a storm approaches). But its strength would have been severely compromised without the agonizing treatment of properly setting the broken bone.

Why is your messed up man in pain? Why does he have to endure sickness and suffering? I don't know. But God does. This we do know: God will use the pain to heal weakness in your man—weaknesses that may be invisible to the human eye. Think of your messed up man in the context of the three truths I learned from Jerry Bridges:

1. God can change his circumstances at any time.
2. God knows what He is doing in your loved one, and this way is the very best way—even if it's painful.
3. God loves you, and he loves your messed up man even more than you realize. God loves your man enough to pull back on his shoulder blades until the broken bones are set.

Ladies, regardless of the suffering your man may be experiencing, you can join God in His work of healing and restoration. But first, let's take a look at an example of how not to treat your man in the midst of his affliction.

TINA ❧ "So Satan went out from the presence of the Lord and afflicted Job with painful sores from the soles of his feet to the crown of his head. Then Job took a piece of broken pottery and scraped himself with it as he sat among the ashes" (Job 2:7–8 NIV).

It's a heartbreaking picture, and I shiver at the thought of it. As his friends sat with him, watching in silence, Job relieved himself from the itch of his sores as best he could. He lost it all—his health declined rapidly, camels and donkeys stolen, farm hands and servants murdered, sheep and herdsmen burned up, and children killed in a windstorm. But what about his wife?

Amid the loss of his entire household, Job's wife at least remained. How did she cope? Like her husband, she lost her home, her servants, and most importantly, her children.

A woman's home is her nest. It's the place she sets in order, and in it raises her children. It's where she sets photos of special moments, passed-down antiques, finger-painted artwork, and necklaces made of macaroni. This nest is where she entertains friends, embraces good and bad, and stores up treasured memories. As a wife, I'd consider the devastation of losing my home to be more than enough. But then to lose my children—as a parent, I can't imagine the suffering.

In the midst of her own grief, had Job's wife given up on God? A scene in Scripture stands out. I picture it unfolding this way.

There Job sits, scraping at his weeping sores with a piece of crockery. Busy about her chores, his wife sees him sitting there, wounded far deeper than the physical marks of his illness. Back and forth she paces, willing herself to stay busy. Her thoughts race; her emotions swell. She strives to control them, but finally she reaches the breaking point and storms toward her husband. Can this monstrosity in front of her even be him? Blood and puss ooze from the body of a man she barely recognizes. "Are you still maintaining your integrity?" she screams at him. "Curse God and die!"

Has her faith left? Is this misplaced anger? Or is she simply sick of it all? She suffers too. She grieves. She understands the ache of Job's loss because it is her own as well.

What does she mean by "curse God and die"? This statement confuses Bible scholars as well as ordinary readers, because the Hebrew word for "curse" can also be translated "bless," and involves the idea of kneeling.[2] The Hebrew has a double meaning. It's similar to the modern saying "You're so bad!" *Bad* can mean bad, but it can also mean good.

Let's suppose Mrs. Job put it this way: "Are you still holding on to your God? After all you're suffering? Why don't you just get it over with? Reject Him so you can die!" Did she believe that if Job threw in the towel, his suffering would end; that if he cursed God, God would end his misery?

Then again, let's suppose she said, "Are you still maintaining your innocence? Why don't you get it over with? Fall before God and repent of your sins so you can die." Did she believe that if Job confessed his sin, kneeling before God, that God would bless Job by releasing him through death?

Francis Andersen, in his commentary on Job, puts it this way, "She [Mrs. Job] sees death as the only good remaining for Job. He should pray to God (lit. 'bless') to be allowed to die, or even *curse God* in order to die, an indirect way of committing suicide."[3] Job's wife is the only one who can interpret the meaning.

Either way, the question is, could she really see Job's suffering? Ladies, when the man in our life suffers, are we so wrapped up in what his suffering is doing to us that we can't see him? Do we curse him with our actions and words because we're tired of the burden? Once we've answered that question, then perhaps we're ready to move forward in dealing with our circumstances.

Facing the Battle

Job battled illness, but other men in the Bible suffered in other ways. How did the women in their lives cope?

Mephibosheth, son of Jonathan and grandson to King Saul, was only five years old when his life changed. After receiving news that Mephibosheth's father and grandfather died in battle and the family might be in danger, the nurse panicked, picked up Mephibosheth, and then fell as she fled with him. The fall broke his legs, and from that day on he was lame in both feet.

How did the fall affect the nurse who cared for Mephibosheth? We simply don't know. Where was the boy's mother? More than likely Rizpah, who is believed to be the mother of Mephibosheth, had already passed away. "The nurse carried him to Lo-debar among the mountains of Gilead, where he was brought up by Machir, son of Ammiel."[4]

We see other men in the Bible besides Mephibosheth and Job struck with various afflictions. The Lord told King Hezekiah, "Put your house in order, because you are going to die; you will not recover" (2 Kings 20:1 NIV). What if that were us? What would we do with such distressing news? Like Hezekiah, most of us would turn our face to the wall, weep, and cry out to God.

In his later years, my father turned his life around and lived to give back, go to church, and read the Bible. In 2006, at the age of seventy-eight, he became ill. During heart surgery his kidneys failed and he eventually contracted MRSA. The deadly staph infection is difficult to battle even for a young person in a healthy body, let alone for an elderly man facing dialysis. We held on to hope that dad could fight the illness, but eventually his body gave out and we received the news, "It won't be long now."

When I was a little girl, my father used to pay me a quarter to wash his feet. At first it was an easy way to put money in my pocket, but as I grew older, I tired of it and stopped. The truth is, my father's feet hurt after spending much of the day standing at work. Later in life he contracted diabetes, and that added to the pain in his feet.

Throughout the years I watched my mother rub lotion on my dad's aching soles. I didn't think much about it until I sat in the hospital room waiting for Dad to take his last breath. Surrounded by machines and tubes, he gave me one last hug, squeezed my hand, and then drifted off into a deep sleep.

During our vigil, my mother and I sang. Our harmonizing drifted out into the hallway. In the heart of my father's passing, he heard singing. And then it happened. My mother took a bottle of lotion and squeezed a quarter-sized amount into her hands, warmed it by rubbing her palms together, and then, picking up one of Dad's feet, anointed it with the soothing cream. Tears trickled down my cheeks as I watched Mom massage and stroke my father's feet the way she had done so many times throughout the years. It was a beautiful picture of blessing.

For the first time in my life I understood what it looked like to love to the very end, bless to the very end, and give to the very end. My mother rubbed Dad's feet one final time, and it crushed my heart into a million pieces.

In that instant I looked deep at myself and realized my selfishness. My husband has needed surgery on his feet and I hadn't lifted a finger to care for them. Dave doesn't live with a chronic illness; he hasn't been diagnosed with a life-threatening disease, yet he lives with a pain that is unknown to me. I see it as he limps his way up the stairs. Now I ask God to help me recognize my husband's moments of need. What can I do? How can I bless? How can I minister?

Women don't always see the truth in their man's suffering. Sometimes we forget he is sick or in pain, especially if the disease isn't outwardly apparent and we've lived with it for a long time. In Job's case, it was difficult to miss, yet his wife still couldn't see. Rather than help Job find comfort, she felt it better for him to simply end his life. Our own grief, like hers, often keeps us from ministering to another person.

Ladies, we face the battle too. We long for a cure, freedom, stability, a healthy man in our life, and a normal life as a couple, or family, or friends. We have no idea how to cope with the daily struggles of living with a man who suffers from an illness or disability.

I once took my ten- and twelve-year-old sons to play laser tag. Our competitors were three large men in black hoodies. They looked like something out of the bad part of an inner city. *Oh, no,* I thought, *we're in trouble.* No one cracked a smile as the hoodies fell over their stern looks.

Upon entering the dark room, I grabbed my sons and began the pep talk moms give their children. "We can do this! We can beat these guys. Now let's go!" I said with conviction, then charged in, tripped over my feet, and fell flat on my face. Everyone heard the loud *flump.*

"Mom! What are you doing?" came the whispers. *Trying to get the bad guys,* I said to myself, nose dug deep in the hard floor. My sons picked me up. "This way," they said. Shots and lights flashed through the dark room. I held a laser tag gun but had no idea what to do with it. My boys shot like little army men. I cowered behind them, tucked my head, hid in crannies, and threw my body to the floor to escape enemy fire.

The truth is, I had no idea how to fight this kind of battle. Eventually

I recognized my ineptness and surrendered my aching body to my
skilled sons. In the end, we won the battle. Actually my two sons won.
Those beady-eyed, hooded men had no idea they were playing against
two preteens skilled in video games.

The battle your man faces is difficult. You want to help, and you can
in so many ways. But you cannot fight the battle for him. Better to tuck
your head and tail behind God and let Him take the lead. Perhaps the
fighting won't lead to healing, but it can lead to peace, comfort, rest,
endurance, strength, and perseverance as you walk with suffering men.

How to Add Quality of Life

There are three things we can learn from Mephibosheth, Hezekiah,
and most certainly Job.

1. Live Life

Mephibosheth lost his entire family. As a child, he suffered an acci-
dent that changed the whole course of his life. He was raised in a desolate
place and stripped of his royalty. But in the end, King David searched
him out and restored him to his rightful position. David couldn't give
Mephibosheth back his ability to walk, but he could give him back his
father's and grandfather's land.

Is that when Mephibosheth started living? No. Somewhere along the
road, Mephibosheth married. He had a helpmate, a companion, someone to walk with him. This woman, whom we know nothing about, married a crippled man, and together they conceived a son who would one
day carry on his father's name. Mephibosheth didn't put life on hold—
he moved forward. And the woman in his life helped him do that.

Find a way to live and enjoy life with the physically messed up man
in your life—in all circumstances.

2. Set Things Right

The Lord told Hezekiah to put his affairs in order. If you live with
a man who has a chronic illness or a life-threatening disease, you may
need to do the following:

Prioritize. Decide what's most important in life right now. For starters, if God isn't at the top of your list, then perhaps it's time to rethink your priorities. Do you need to clean the house or rub lotion on feet? Make time for the most important things.

Live a quality-filled life. Find things to do that bring laughter, peace, and joy to the sick man in your life. Acknowledging that there may be limitations, nevertheless, reach out to do something he enjoys.

My twenty-three-year-old nephew died a few years back after a long battle with cystic fibrosis. I miss him so much. A few months before his death, he called me to share how he and a friend got kicked out of the hospital.

"Kicked out!" I said.

He laughed. "Well, *she* did." He had convinced her to come and play her tuba for him in his hospital room. Anyone who's played the tuba knows how the sound travels. My nephew giggled about his adventure and treasured his quality time with a special friend. Who knew the value a few simple tuba notes would bring to a dying young man?

Get ready. You never know what a day will bring. Have you said those words you've always wanted to say? Taken time to tie up loose ends? Don't put things off or live in a mess-filled atmosphere. There's peace in knowing we have our affairs in order. After Hezekiah poured out his heart to the Lord, he was given fifteen more years to live. Even with those added years, I envision Hezekiah getting his affairs in order. He was bound to honor God by doing so.

3. Be Present

When Job's friends heard about his troubles, they agreed to visit Job together. They desired to "sympathize with him and comfort him. When they saw him from a distance, they could hardly recognize him;

they began to weep aloud, and they tore their robes and sprinkled dust on their heads" (Job 2:11–12 NIV).

At first, Job's friends had no idea how badly he suffered. When they caught their first glimpse of him at a distance, they broke down, because they had already determined to open their eyes to his suffering and their hearts to comforting him. Job's wife did neither. Had she truly seen her husband, she would have done as his friends did. "They sat on the ground with him for seven days and seven nights. No one said a word to him, because they saw how great his suffering was" (v. 13 NIV).

Ladies, sometimes a man's simply knowing that you see his suffering and that you care may be enough to sustain him during his difficult time. Simply being there expresses your deep affection and love.

Take Action

DAVE ✼ Job set some examples you can practice with your man or do by yourself. Good things will happen as you emulate Job with these six simple principles.

1. Turn Whining into Worship

Earlier Tina mentioned worship. Worship may not have been easy for a man who had lost everything except his faith. We know Job's faith survived because his reaction to his devastating loss was to worship God: "Then Job arose and tore his robe and shaved his head, and he fell to the ground and worshiped. He said, 'Naked I came from my mother's womb, and naked I shall return there. The Lord gave and the Lord has taken away. Blessed be the name of the Lord'" (Job 1:20–21). Let me encourage you and your messed up man, should he be willing, to begin to worship God from your place of brokenness.

Tina shares a dramatic story from her work as a music therapist for hospice. One day, as she prepared to leave the hospice floor at the hospital, a nurse called her back to work with a patient in respiratory arrest.

Music therapists use music to match the beat of a patient's heart rate, and as the therapist slows down the beat of music, most of the time the heart rate follows, as well as the breathing. At the start of the process, the patient's wife shouted, "Sing 'Amazing Grace'!" Deciding to minister rather than work, Tina sang "Amazing Grace." The patient's distress was overwhelming. He could hardly take in air, and his chest heaved while his wife wept.

Right in the middle of "Amazing Grace," the wife once more blurted out, "Sing 'Jesus Loves Me'!" Tina, switched gears and sang, "Yes, Jesus loves me." Tears streamed down the man's cheeks as he sang with her, "Yes, Jesus loves me." His words were broken and he could hardly say them, but in that moment, he worshiped the God who was about to take him home. Whatever you're facing . . . worship.

2. Accept Your Trial

The second principle is to move into an acceptance of the trial. "Afterward Job opened his mouth and cursed the day of his birth" (Job 3:1). Job recognized that his life was no longer marked by blessing but that he had entered into a time of testing. He realized the full impact of what he was now experiencing. Compared to the blessing he had previously enjoyed, Job concluded that he would be better off had he died at birth. Those of us who have suffered great loss can relate to Job's lament, "Why is light given to him who suffers, and life to the bitter of soul, who long for death, but there is none" (Job 3:20–21).

There is a strange comfort in finally accepting one's circumstances. Some of you may have mixed feelings about this, as some churches teach us to reject suffering, sickness, and disease. I'm not asking you to give up, but rather to release your situation into the hands of God. When we accept, we release. When we release, we're no longer trying to control. Perhaps then God can finally take the lead. That's when we find freedom to cope.

3. Understand Your Value

Throughout the book of Job, we see Job insisting that his change of circumstance is not due to sin. He maintains his innocence—his value, if you will. Difficult days take their toll, but we are refreshed as we remember our value to God and to each other. God does love us, God does love the sick man in our life, and God does care. We are worth fighting for, and that is something we need to know if we are to walk through this shadowy valley of death and sickness.

4. Listen to God

The fourth principle is to move into a place of listening. Job was upset and made some pretty startling accusations toward God. (Haven't we done the same in our own suffering?) Following a lengthy rebuke by God, we see these words spill from Job's lips: "I will ask You, and You instruct me" (Job 42:4). Ah! Job was now ready to surrender his attitude and suffering to God. Let me challenge you to ask God for His perspective on your situation. Can you grow still and listen to His words? Will you attempt to receive His words, and with them, comfort and rest?

5. Switch Your Focus

The fifth principle is to begin focusing on others. But how, when we're suffering so much? "The Lord restored the fortunes of Job when he prayed for his friends" (Job 42:10). Do you see it? In the midst of his pain, Job took his eyes off himself and prayed for others.

How can you help the man in your life turn his eyes away from his situation to focus on others? As a woman, you can come alongside your man and walk with him through those moments. That is what Jesus did on the cross—kept us uppermost in the midst of his own suffering—and it's what we'll do when He lives in us.

6. Wait for Restoration

The final principle is to move into a place of restoration. "The Lord restored the fortunes of Job when he prayed for his friends, and the Lord increased all that Job had twofold" (Job 42:10). In the verses that conclude the book of Job, we see an amazing restoration of Job's life and fortune.

I can't guarantee that your circumstances will change in the dramatic fashion that Job's did as he moved through his six steps. What I can guarantee is that you will change.

TINA ❧ When we read these words from someone who suffered a great deal, our hearts can't help but leap as well: "Once I knew only darkness and stillness. . . . My life was without past or future . . . but a little word from the fingers of another fell into my hand that clutched at emptiness, and my heart leaped to the rapture of living."[5]

Though Helen Keller was born with the ability to see and hear, at nineteen months old she contracted an illness that left her deaf and blind. However, through the help of one person, Helen's life changed. She never regained her hearing or sight; instead, she received hope in a distress-filled life.

What faith, encouragement, tender touch, or spoken word can you place in the palm of your suffering man? Can you point him to the One who can replace his emptiness with "the rapture of living"? And can you take hold of that overwhelming joy as well?

To that end, in the words of the apostle Paul, "We [will not stop] praying for you. We [will] continually ask God to fill you with the knowledge of his will through all the wisdom and understanding that the Spirit gives, so that you may live a life worthy of the Lord and please him in every way: bearing fruit in every good work, growing in the knowledge of God, being strengthened with all power according to his glorious might so that you may have great endurance and patience" (Col. 1:9–11 NIV).

Six Principles to Practice for a Healthier Relationship

1. Turn whining into worship.
2. Accept your trial.
3. Understand your value.
4. Listen to God.
5. Switch your focus.
6. Wait for restoration.

Moving Beyond the Mess

1. Read Job 1:20–22. Consider Job's state of mind. Where did his thoughts turn? Relate his reaction to how we respond to tragedy.
2. Dave mentioned three facts about God: God is sovereign, God is wise, and God is love. How can these truths comfort those living with a man facing illness?
3. Have you, or someone you know, lived with a man who had a chronic illness? What difficulties were faced? How did you or they minister to the sick man?
4. Consider Job's wife and her reaction to losing her children and home and then having to care for Job. What difficulties might she have faced? What did she mean by "Curse God and die"?
5. Read over Dave's list of things to do when living with a sick man (turn whining into worship, accept your trial, etc.). Which one do you, or would you, have the most difficulty with? Why?
6. *Moving to a healthier place:* How can we come alongside women who care for men with chronic illnesses? Identify specific ways to meet emotional needs, physical needs, and so on.

May the man in your life find healing, and may you find strength to comfort, minister, and offer peace.

6

Elijah

A Pitiful Prophet

Depression is a prison where you are both the suffering prisoner and the cruel jailer.
Dorothy Rowe, Depression:
The Way Out of Your Prison

Elijah gazed across the vast panorama and sucked in a deep breath. His servant looked as well, then turned back to Elijah.

"Stay here," Elijah said, stepping away. The crunch of dry ground underfoot seemed louder than normal.

"But master, where are you going?" The servant moved toward Elijah.

"No, stay here."

Elijah set out across the open desert. Standing on the edge of the town, the servant watched as the prophet dwindled to a speck and then vanished into the arid landscape.

Hours passed. Sweat slid down Elijah's nose as the sun, now at its zenith, beat down on his head. Silence hung in the air like a curtain.

Where are your slayers, Jezebel? Elijah glanced back over his shoulder.

The distance held only hot haze and shimmering mirage. No one followed. Elijah shuffled onward.

More hours rolled by; more dry, desolate miles passed underfoot. The sun slid westward from high overhead as Elijah paused to reach one more time for his goatskin water pouch, uncork it, and raise it to his mouth. A few drops were all that was left—enough to wet his parched lips, and no more.

I can't do this . . . I can't do this.

A lone juniper beckoned in the distance, its shadow stretched out invitingly across the hot sands. Two hundred yards . . . two hundred feet . . . a few more steps . . . Elijah collapsed beneath the tree.

I have had enough, Lord. Please take my life. I am useless. Worthless— no better than my ancestors.

Afternoon waned into evening. The sun was setting, but Elijah cared nothing for the orange and gold hues shimmering off the desert's edge. He was exhausted from his day's travel, and his emotional state left him with one desire: for his pain to end.

DAVE ❦ I find it amazing how God often orders my day. As Tina headed off to do an interview with our local newspaper one morning, I decided that I would get a quick haircut before I started writing. I had been working on this chapter, and the subject of depression and suicide was fresh in my mind. Less than two weeks before, celebrated comedian Robin Williams had committed suicide. Since then, the country had been talking about depression, and I myself had given a biblical exposition on it the previous Sunday. I was thinking about what I wanted to write for this chapter, but first I needed a haircut. (It's not unusual for me to come up with an excuse not to write, even if it's just a haircut.)

There is a local hair styling chain near my house that I've been using for a couple years—the kind of place where they get you in and out in ten to fifteen minutes. I don't go often enough to know any of the stylists, and this particular day I was assigned to Jane. We were barely past discussing the weather when Jane told me her fiancé had died last September. I expressed my condolences and asked how she was coping. After a long pause, she said, "Do you think people who commit suicide go to heaven?"

Forty minutes later, my hair was the shortest it has been since I was in the Navy, but God gave me the chance to share with Jane how she could begin the process of healing from her fiancé's suicide. Both Robin Williams and Jane's fiancé have a connection with one of the most powerful men of God in the Bible—Elijah.

The FADE

God shows us in Scripture that even the most stable men fall into despair.

[Elijah] was afraid and arose and ran for his life and came to Beersheba, which belongs to Judah, and left his servant there. But he himself went a day's journey into the wilderness, and came and sat down under a juniper tree; and he requested for himself that he might die, and said, "It is enough; now, O Lord, take my life, for I am not better than my fathers." He lay down and slept under a juniper tree. (1 Kings 19:3–5)

I call this Elijah's FADE. (Be patient. I'll break out this acronym in a bit.) While we can only speculate how the story really unfolded, it's a remarkable change of position. We find our hero, Elijah, sleeping under a tree, despairing, defeated, and wanting to die. He sees no reason to continue his miserable life. Stick a fork in him—he's done! What's remarkable is that in the two chapters that precede 1 Kings 19, we see nothing but victory for Elijah. He is a mighty man of God. Nothing is impossible or too big for him.

Seven Supernatural Signs

The seventeenth and eighteenth chapters of 1 Kings describe seven supernatural signs that God produced by the hand of Elijah:

1. At the word of Elijah, the dew and rain stopped.
2. During the drought, when food and water became scarce, God
   provided for Elijah at the brook Cherith. Ravens brought him
   bread and meat every morning and evening.
3. The brook eventually dried up, and God sent Elijah to a widow in
   Zarephath. God miraculously caused the widow's small amount
   of flour and oil to last through all the days of the drought.
4. When the widow's son died, God brought him back to life
   through Elijah's prayer.
5. Elijah called fire down from heaven and defeated 850 false
   prophets.
6. The rain miraculously returned as Elijah prayed.
7. Elijah ran really far (about seventeen miles) really, *really* fast.

A common element connects these seven amazing acts of God: Elijah
wasn't just a powerful man; he was a common man empowered by the
almighty God. As I look back over 1 Kings, chapters 17 and 18, I count
no fewer than ten times where the text declares the presence of either
the word of the Lord or the hand of the Lord. The message is clear:
Elijah was empowered by God as he submitted to the activity of God.

Noticeably absent when we reach chapter 19 are the terms "word of
the Lord" and "hand of the Lord." Chapter 19 begins, "Now Ahab told
Jezebel all that Elijah had done, and how he had killed all the prophets
with the sword. Then Jezebel sent a messenger to Elijah, saying, 'So
may the gods do to me and even more, if I do not make your life as the
life of one of them by tomorrow about this time.' And he was afraid"
(vv. 1–3).

Jezebel threatens Elijah, and absent the word of the Lord, Elijah
runs. Only this time Elijah runs in his own power, not God's. Elijah's
power fades, and so does Elijah.

I see four elements in Elijah's FADE, and they are common to all of
us, including your messed up man. God has a perspective on each of
them.

Fear: "And he was afraid and arose and ran for his life" (1 Kings 19:3).

- God's perspective: "Perfect love casts out fear" (1 John 4:18).

Alone-ness: "[He] came to Beersheba, which belongs to Judah, and left his servant there. But he himself went a day's journey into the wilderness" (1 Kings 19:3–4).

- God's perspective: "It is not good for the man to be alone" (Gen. 2:18).

Despair: "[He] sat down under a juniper tree; and he requested for himself that he might die" (1 Kings 19:4).

- God's perspective: "Now may the God of hope fill you with all joy and peace in believing, so that you will abound in hope by the power of the Holy Spirit" (Rom. 15:13).

Exhaustion: "He lay down and slept under a juniper tree" (1 Kings 19:5).

- God's perspective: "Awake, sleeper, and arise from the dead, and Christ will shine on you" (Eph. 5:14).

The Deliverance

These four elements of the FADE are your enemy, and they are the enemy of your man. But they can be rejected through the five Ts that Elijah experienced, and you can help. Your voice, your touch, and your love, in partnership with God, can help break through and reverse the FADE. How? Look at the way God delivered Elijah as he sat beneath the juniper tree.

1. Touched by God

[Elijah] lay down and slept under a juniper tree; and behold, there was an angel touching him, and he said to him, 'Arise, eat.' Then he looked and behold, there was at his head a bread

cake baked on hot stones, and a jar of water. So he ate and
drank and lay down again." (1 Kings 19:5–6)

In the midst of Elijah's despair, an angel touched him. God touched
him! Your messed up man needs to feel the touch of God, and he
needs to feel your touch as well. One of the most intimate experiences
of prayer that I have ever had is waking up from sleep, in a darkened
room, during the midst of deep depression, only to feel Tina's hand on
my head and to hear Tina's soft words speaking a prayer of deliverance
over me.

2. Travel to God

> So he arose and ate and drank, and went in the strength of that
> food forty days and forty nights to Horeb, the mountain of
> God. (1 Kings 19:8)

Elijah traveled to the mountain of God where he would meet God in
person. The journey to God isn't a long one. It may be a meeting with
your pastor, an evening at Celebrate Recovery,[1] or just a prayer or Scripture that you pray over your man. Tina and I have had many of these
journeys—trips to the mountain of God where we retreat into God's
love, acceptance, and restoration.

3. Talk to God

> After the earthquake [came] a fire, but the Lord was not in the
> fire; and after the fire a sound of a gentle blowing. When Elijah
> heard it, he wrapped his face in his mantle and went out and
> stood in the entrance of the cave. And behold, a voice came
> to him and said, "What are you doing here, Elijah?" (1 Kings
> 19:12–13)

Elijah heard God not in a great wind, nor in a violent earthquake, nor even in a mighty fire. He heard the voice of God in a gentle breeze—a still, small voice. Your voice can be that gentle voice by

speaking love, acceptance, and encouragement into your man's cloud of despair. Sometimes the best thing you can say is, "I believe in you," "We're going to make it," or better yet, "I love you." Continue to affirm your love.

4. Turn to God's Purpose
> The Lord said to him, "Go, return on your way to the wilderness of Damascus." (1 Kings 19:15)

Elijah had a purpose, and God reminded him of that purpose. He was to return, and he was to start acting like a prophet. He was to anoint kings and prophets. One root of a man's depression is a lack of purpose—to not understand that life holds meaning. Tina has often reminded me of how God has used me in the past and how He is using me in the present. As men, one little criticism, like Elijah experienced, can send us running. A word of encouragement is sometimes all we need to refocus.

These first four Ts are something you play a part in, ways you can partner with God in bringing hope, healing, and deliverance to your messed up man. The fifth and final T is God's province alone.

5. Taken by God
> As they were going along and talking, behold, there appeared a chariot of fire and horses of fire which separated the two of them. And Elijah went up by a whirlwind to heaven. (2 Kings 2:11)

I love Elijah's surprise ending! The very one who had asked for God to take his life . . . never dies! That's right—Elijah never tasted death.

I don't know what your ending will be like, but God does. He has already planned it. I don't know if you will experience a chariot of fire or something far less dramatic. Far beyond the end of our life, today can be the day that you and your messed up man are taken by God—taken by His love, by His power, by His glory!

Four Ways to Minister to Someone Battling Depression

1. **Touch**—Find ways to express your love through touch. Lay hands on your man and pray, rub his head, embrace him gently, take a walk with him and hold hands. Reassure him that he is not alone.

2. **Travel**—Encourage him to attend church with you, go to Celebrate Recovery, seek out a pastor, go with him to counseling, get him out of the house, take a drive, and travel with him through this process toward healing.

3. **Talk**—Keep lines of communication open, be transparent, allow him to express his feelings, empathize with his suffering, and affirm him not only in his progress but also in his work. Affirm him as a man. Affirm your love for him. Ask what you can do to help him.

4. **Turn**—Continue to direct his eyes toward the Lord, who has a perfect plan for his life. Model positive behavior; turn his negative thoughts away by speaking a word of encouragement. Turn his thoughts toward the Word of God and positive thinking. Point out his blessings, the things that are going well for him and your family.

TINA ❧ As a prophet of the Lord, Elijah never married; at least Scripture gives no evidence that he had a wife. However, during his life, two women impacted him in a great way. One woman gave life while the other tried to take it away. One woman sparked purpose and meaning while the other stirred fear and despair. One woman was gracious and kind while the other was callous and cold.

Elijah met the widow of Zarephath after he confronted King Ahab. Let's start at the beginning. Ahab reigned over Israel. He was powerful not only due to his position but also because he married Jezebel. Jezebel, a king's daughter, kept company with four hundred fifty prophets of Baal and 400 prophets of Asherah. Because of her, Ahab did more evil in the eyes of the Lord than all the kings who came before him.

One day Elijah faced this king and declared a drought (1 Kings 17:1). From that moment on the skies closed up, and Elijah ran like a fugitive. Jezebel sent soldiers to find Elijah and in the process killed other prophets of the Lord.

Now we come to the third and fourth of Elijah's miracles in Dave's list. The Lord directed Elijah to Zarephath in Phoenicia—right to Jezebel's neck of the woods, where people fell at the feet of false idols. As he made his way into the city, tired from walking the vast, dry land, Elijah came upon a woman picking up sticks and asked her for a drink of water. She kindly took care of his request.

One might take Elijah's encounter with the widow as a coincidence. But listen to what the Lord told Elijah: "Go at once to Zarephath in the region of Sidon and stay there. I have directed a widow there to supply you with food" (1 Kings 17:9 NIV).

Did the widow know Elijah was coming? Did God speak to her and tell her what to do when Elijah arrived? The Hebrew word for *directed* means "to command, charge, give orders." God appointed a widow to help Elijah, and she didn't even know it. Had she known, her greeting to Elijah would have perhaps looked like this: "Are you the one the Lord sent? I've been waiting."

God's hand settled upon her and gave her a willing and agreeable heart to help Elijah. Without the involvement of the Holy Spirit, this encounter would have been just another encounter.

This widow prepared the last of her food for Elijah. Because of her obedience to God, the jar of flour was not used up and the jug of oil never ran dry. God took care of them both.

Something else about this passage struck my heart. Let's look at Jesus's words in Luke 4. "I assure you that there were many widows in Israel in Elijah's time, when the sky was shut for three and a half years and there was a severe famine throughout the land. Yet Elijah was not sent to any of them, but to a widow in Zarephath in the region of Sidon" (vv. 25–26 NIV).

This passage moved me to tears. First, many women lost their husbands due to the famine; they were now widows. Second, God could have sent Elijah to any one of those widows. And last—get this picture—the widow of Zarephath was *chosen*.

The Chosen

My son asked, "Why are you crying, Mom?" I needed a moment to compose myself. God chose this particular widow to minister to Elijah. According to Jesus, God could have picked any one of the widows who lost their husbands during the three-and-a-half-year famine. But God chose her.

When I first became a pastor's wife, I thought, *God, really? I hope you know what you're doing. I, who received a negative three in hospitality on my spiritual gift survey, a pastor's wife?* At retreats and conferences for pastors' wives, I heard women say, "I was called to be a pastor's wife." I never felt called. What was wrong with me?

Then came the eye-opening moment at one retreat when a senior woman said, "I was never called to be a pastor's wife, but I was called to be *his* wife." Finally! Someone said it. But was I called to be my husband's wife? I didn't know. However, whether from my own personal decision, a calling, or a choosing by God as with the widow of Zarephath, I was committed and knitted.

Okay, that might sound corny, but the definition of knitted is "to join closely and firmly, as members or parts."[2] David and I were now intertwined, braided, and twisted together. So perhaps I *was* chosen to partner with the messed up man in my life.

My dear sisters, here's the question: Do we think God can do today what He did back then? Can we believe that perhaps by some miracle we were chosen for the messed up man in our life? And he us? That God had a purpose and plan for the two of us from the very beginning?

Elijah lived with the widow for a while. Sometime later her son grew ill and stopped breathing. She said to Elijah, "What do you have against me, man of God? Did you come to remind me of my sin and kill my son?" Elijah took her son to the upper room, lay on him, and prayed, "Lord my God, let this boy's life return to him!" The Lord heard Elijah's cry, the boy's life returned to him, and Elijah carried him alive back down from the room and gave him to his mother. "Look, your son is alive," he said. The woman responded, "Now I know that you are a man of God and that the word of the Lord in your mouth is truth" (1 Kings 17:17–24, my rendering).

Here we see why God chose this widow and sent Elijah to her: not just to bring her boy back to life, but very importantly, to open the eyes of a widow who lived in a land where idol worship ruled and bring eternal life to her. Through her encounter with Elijah, the widow understood the word of the Lord as *truth*.

I suppose the bond between Elijah and the widow caused a bittersweet departure.

The Jezebel Effect

Jezebel: daughter of a king, married to a king, strong leader, master manipulator, and mass murderer. She too was a woman who changed Elijah's life.

After Elijah left the widow, he traveled back to Samaria and settled a huge issue: which God was greater, his or Jezebel's. It would be worth your time to read the story in 1 Kings 18–19. After Elijah's God proved to be the one true God, Elijah killed all the prophets of Baal, whom Jezebel worshiped.

Big move! There's nothing worse than a woman scorned. Fuming, Jezebel sent a message to Elijah: "So may the gods do to me and even more, if I do not make your life as the life of one of them [Baal's prophets] by tomorrow about this time" (1 Kings 19:2). Based on Jezebel's track record, Elijah understood one thing—she meant what she said.

Jezebel could not tolerate Elijah. Ladies, does the depressed man in our life see us that way—as someone who incites fear rather than instills hope? Someone who is callous and cold toward his state of mind? Though we may not be trying to kill him, are we bringing him life?

The widow of Zarephath and Queen Jezebel both impacted Elijah in significant—but very different—ways. Do you see yourself in either woman?

Do Not Fear

Though facing depression, the man in your life isn't alone, nor does his depression mean he will never amount to anything. Below are a few names you might recognize of men who've struggled with depression.

+ Buzz Aldrin (American astronaut)
+ Wolfgang Amadeus Mozart (classical musician)
+ Terry Bradshaw, Earl Campbell (athletes)
+ Marlon Brando, Harrison Ford (actors)
+ Teddy Roosevelt, Abraham Lincoln (politicians)
+ Drew Carey, Dick Clark (television personalities)
+ Mark Twain, Ernest Hemingway (authors)
+ Billy Joel, Bob Dylan (singers)
+ Greg Louganis (Olympic medalist)
+ Charles Schultz (author of Peanuts)
+ Sir Isaac Newton (physicist)

It's important for women to look at their messed up man not as weak and feeble but as God sees him: someone with the power to achieve great things; someone who, with support, encouragement, and love, can get up every morning and step into life, even though he doesn't feel like it. And remember, even though his life at times feels unbalanced, yours doesn't have to.

Are you afraid? Are you concerned? Suppose God, in His great wisdom, chooses to do something unexpected in your life: change you, and use your connection with the messed up man to do it.

In his book *Talent Is Never Enough*, John Maxwell quotes an attorney: "Your life does not get better by chance, it gets better by change."[3] In my own husband's bouts of depression, who knew that by His working in Dave's life, God would change mine as well? I confess, I often tired of his depressed days, ignored the behavior, acted as if his mood didn't affect me, didn't extend sympathy or empathy, and pretended nothing was happening. That behavior is easy to accomplish when we don't understand the suffering. Through Dave's depression, I learned more about myself. On his dark days, I learned patience, endurance, and how to keep from personalizing those moments. I learned how to listen while he paced the floor and to process what triggered his depressed thoughts. I learned how to pat his back, rub his head, and affirm—though I never truly understood how he felt.

Understand: "to know the meaning of something, to know how something works, to know how one thinks, feels, or behaves."[4] Wouldn't life be nice if we understood everything we go through? Fear is in the unknown. What do we do with the unknown? Do we stare it down, sweep it under the rug, or tuck tail and run?

We need to hear the words Elijah heard during his despair: "Go out and stand on the mountain in the presence of the Lord, for the Lord is about to pass by" (1 Kings 19:11 NIV).

Wow, the Lord is about to pass by! Imagine a young child standing on her tiptoes to see her favorite celebrity. Her tiny head bobs up and down. Her eyes gleam with anticipation. "He's coming!" she shouts.

If you knew the Lord was about to pass by, where would you run? What heights would you climb? How far would you go? How much work would you do to get to Him? When Elijah climbed to his position, the winds blew, rocks cracked, the ground shook, rains poured, and mountains split in two. "But God, you said you were about to pass by. I don't get it," I'd say in fear, without understanding. Would I have waited as Elijah did or scrambled down the mountain? My spirit says yes, but my gut tells me no.

"After the earthquake came a fire, but the Lord was not in the fire. And after the fire came a gentle whisper" (v. 12 NIV). When Elijah heard the whisper, he stood at the mouth of the cave. He wrapped himself in his furry cloak—and waited. I admire that about Elijah. Earlier he was despairing and depressed; he felt defeated. But on the mountain, waiting for the Lord to pass by, he could stand in the face of disaster.

There's something about knowing the Lord is coming. It brings hope, an extra boost of energy we've needed. It's like the dash of grit that helps us walk that extra block when our legs feel like mush, push through another hour of work when our eyelids hang to our knees, or rise at the crack of dawn on cold, rainy days when we'd rather pull the covers over our head. *Get up! He's coming.*

When we silence everything around us till the only thing left is the faint sound of a whisper, a miracle happens. The world stops and chaos is edged out. We don't hear anything but the voice, the whisper. For women, it might feel like two lovers locking eyes in a romantic moment. Nothing comes between them.

The Lord whispered. Elijah heard. And Elijah shared his burden with the Lord, not realizing that his fear came from not understanding. He believed he was the only survivor of Jezebel's murderous campaign against the Lord's prophets. But with His still, small voice, God revealed that Elijah wasn't alone. God had reserved "seven thousand [prophets] in Israel—all whose knees have not bowed down to Baal and whose mouths have not kissed him" (v. 18 NIV).

You may not understand depression or the devastating impact it has on the men in your life. You're not alone. You may find yourself on a roller coaster of mood swings and meds. You're not alone. You may be holding on to a great deal of fear and very little understanding. You're not alone.

Though God is the only one who understands *all* things, we can hold on to one promise: "For he has not despised or scorned the suffering of the afflicted one; he has not hidden his face from him but has listened to his cry for help" (Ps. 22:24 NIV). Though it feels as if we have been forgotten, God promises that's not the case, and we won't always feel this way. He promises to walk with us, to whisper to us in the storm, to embrace, love, give peace, strengthen, encourage, and so much more. God says we don't have to understand; we just need to be willing to come out and stand in the mouth of the cave. There, He whispers hope.

Though God is the only one who can heal and fix the depressed man in your life, you can take the four Ts Dave spoke of—touch, travel, talk, turn—and begin to apply them to your journey. Decide to make a change in the way you see your situation. Come to see the depressed man as God sees him: as a great man of God with boundless potential and unlimited possibilities. "Encourage one another and build each other up, just as in fact you are doing" (1 Thess. 5:11 NIV).

Through your hardship may you find God in the center of all things. And may He bring healing to the man in your life. May He encourage you each day to fulfill your purpose and plan for your life. May God bring joy in the midst of despair, replace sorrow with gladness, and open doors for hope to flood your homes.

Through this season, recognize that you can choose how you will walk, whether like Jezebel, callous and cruel, or like the widow of Zarephath, willing to nurture and serve. Above all, do not fear. Jesus says, "Peace I leave with you; My peace I give to you; not as the world gives do I give to you. Do not let your heart be troubled, nor let it be fearful" (John 14:27).

Four Ways to Take Care of You

1. **Depersonalize.** Don't personalize anything. The messed up man's despair doesn't need to become yours.

2. **Breathe.** When you find yourself being pulled into your man's despair, take a break. Find time to recharge. Pray, take a walk, talk to a friend, dip in the pool, cook, take a bubble bath, watch a movie, read in a special nook—do whatever relaxes you.

3. **Refuel.** Refuel by staying in God's Word. We gain strength, hope, and power from the Scriptures. God's Word is our mental and spiritual nourishment. Feed yourself well to gain the strength and encouragement you need.

4. **Laugh.** Find ways to laugh and have fun. Though he's struggling, you still need to find ways to enjoy life without feeling guilty. You can empathize with his pain and struggle, but allow yourself the freedom to live.

Moving Beyond the Mess

1. We each look upon depression in a different light. Unless we've experienced the suffering, we may never understand the impact. How would you define depression?

2. Have you or anyone in your family experienced depression? If you feel safe sharing, do so.
3. What stood out to you about Elijah in this chapter?
4. Throughout Elijah's story, food is referenced. Read 1 Kings 17:8 and 19:5–7. How can food strengthen a depressed person? Food can symbolize various kinds of sustenance. God's Word and healthy relationships are two. Can you think of some others? How can a woman help feed the men in her life?
5. Women need a safe place to share their struggles. When the men in our life struggle, it's easy to keep everything in the dark. Read 1 John 1:5–7. What happens when we become transparent and step away from the darkness? In what ways can we walk with women whose men struggle with depression?
6. *Moving to a healthier place:* Consider the "Four Ways to Take Care of You." Which way do you struggle with the most? Why? What steps can you take to move forward to a healthier place?

May God remind you that He loves and cares for you.

---

*May He bring peace and strength to your life and
replace sorrow with joy.*

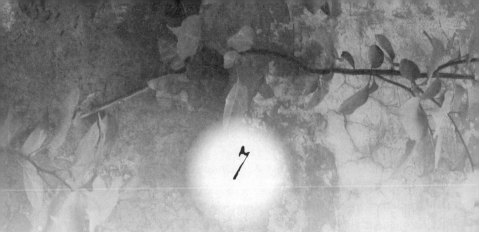

7

Solomon

A Wayward Worshiper

Obey your leaders and submit to them, for they keep
watch over your souls as those who will give an account.
Let them do this with joy and not with grief, for this
would be unprofitable for you.

—Hebrews 13:17

She sits in his chamber, draped across the lush couch. Her dark skin catches the glimmer of light from the flickering candles, and she beckons him, "Kiss me with the kisses of [your] mouth! For your love is better than wine."

He reaches for her. "How beautiful you are, my darling, how beautiful you are! Your eyes are like doves."

A gentle embrace, and then she murmurs, "How handsome you are, my beloved" (Song of Songs 1:1, 15–16).

TINA ✂ This woman goes on to say, "I am lovesick. Let his left hand be under my head and his right hand embrace me." She likens her lover, whom we believe is Solomon, to "a gazelle or a young stag." Wow, I need to meet this Solomon. Okay, who's picturing Chris Hemsworth in the movie *Thor*?

Solomon loved women, and women loved Solomon. Who wouldn't? Throughout the Scriptures, Solomon wows us with his wisdom. In Ecclesiastes he drenches us in deep thought. In Proverbs, he shares practical insights for living life well. And in Song of Solomon, well, let's just say that from what we've read, keep a cool glass of water nearby when reading this book. Solomon's passionate language left his women with no need to wear blush. But that's not all. In addition to his wisdom, knowledge, and passion, Solomon loved God, led prayers and dedications, built a beautiful temple and other buildings, and changed lives.

However, as I said, not only did women love Solomon, but Solomon loved women. Lots of them. And that created a problem.

> Now King Solomon loved many foreign women along with the daughter of Pharaoh: Moabite, Ammonite, Edomite, Sidonian, and Hittite women, from the nations concerning which the Lord had said to the sons of Israel, "You shall not associate with them, nor shall they associate with you, for they will surely turn your heart away after their gods." Solomon held fast to these in love. He had seven hundred wives, princesses, and three hundred concubines, and his wives turned his heart away. (1 Kings 11:1–3)

Solomon's story astounds me. I shake my head and pace the floor over his actions. One look at his magnificent qualities and women all over the world are ready to switch places with the woman on the couch. Amazing—and yet I want to stomp my feet and shout, "Solomon, you're such a—a *man!*" Who are these influential foreign women with the ability to sway a king?

Remember those childhood moments when you heard, "Daddy told you not to do that"? Those cookie-jar incidents, messy mistakes, and wish-you-could-take-it-back moments? Yep. Solomon should have recognized that uh-oh moment when it happened, but he didn't.

When Solomon was old, his wives turned his heart away after other gods; and his heart was not wholly devoted to the Lord his God, as the heart of David his father had been. For Solomon went after Ashtoreth the goddess of the Sidonians and after Milcom the detestable idol of the Ammonites. Solomon did what was evil in the sight of the Lord, and did not follow the Lord fully, as David his father had done. Then Solomon built a high place for Chemosh the detestable idol of Moab, on the mountain which is east of Jerusalem, and for Molech the detestable idol of the sons of Ammon. Thus also he did for all his foreign wives, who burned incense and sacrificed to their gods. (1 Kings 11:4–8)

He did what? There it is—Solomon's moment of abdicating his rightful position as the spiritual leader of his family as well as his kingdom. He married the women as a political move to align Israel with the surrounding countries. Could he not have married the foreign women and still stayed the course and continued to honor God with his actions and leadership? Actually, no. The moment he married, he dishonored God, because God had clearly forbidden him to marry those women.

Solomon married unbelievers who practiced revolting forms of idol worship. The Moabites practiced child sacrifice to their god Chemosh. The Ammonites killed their children and then burned them on the altar of Molech. And the Sidonian devotees of Ashtoreth practiced temple prostitution, among other things.

Yes, we scratch our heads at Solomon's actions. Why, after receiving such blessings from the Lord, did he turn from God in his latter years? Why, after achieving such great feats, would he make such a choice?

Follow the . . . Leader?

"How do I make him lead?" I can't tell you how many times I've sat across from a woman expressing that wish. Women want to shout, "Come on! Step up. You're supposed to be the spiritual leader of this home."

Women have a list of what "spiritual leadership" is supposed to look like. The man will:

+ read the Bible for himself and with the family
+ initiate a family devotion
+ lead in prayer during meals, family prayer times, and other settings
+ grow spiritually and attend men's studies or retreats
+ talk about God, share what God is doing in his life, and testify openly
+ minister to other men

But our expectations can be misleading. Marlena Graves wrote in a *Christianity Today* article,

> Some time ago in the school cafeteria, we ran into a young woman we knew well. Shawn and I had counseled her and her boyfriend the year prior. I asked her about their relationship. "I broke up with him a month or so ago," she said sheepishly. Shawn and I tried to veil our shock.
>
> A few minutes later, I asked her why. "He's just not a spiritual leader," she answered. After we parted ways, Shawn turned to me and said, "I can't help wondering how many otherwise beautiful relationships have ended due to misconceptions about spiritual leadership."[1]

Do women have misconceptions about the way a man should lead his family? With that question asked, let's return to the question of why men relinquish their rights as the spiritual leaders of their homes. Perhaps Dave can shed some light on the matter.

DAVE ❦ Ladies, let me attempt to answer the question, why do men sometimes struggle to be the spiritual leaders in their homes? I'll make it personal: Why do *I* sometimes struggle to be my family's spiritual leader? Please don't hear what I'm about to say as an excuse, but rather, as an attempt to share with you the truth about how many men feel.

1. I'm not always in a good spiritual place. Even when I know what to do, I don't always want to do it. Sometimes I'm in a lousy mood or just lazy. Other times I might feel spiritually weak. The messed up man in your life may not be in a good spiritual place.
2. Leading spiritually sometimes feels hypocritical. My family knows everything about me. They know when I've lost my temper or when I've acted selfishly. I don't want to feel like a hypocrite, and neither does your man. Perhaps he lost his temper at work or home, acted like a Pharisee instead of Christ, or otherwise just plain blew it. To then step into the role of spiritual leader can be difficult.
3. I don't always know what to do. I left home when I was thirteen to attend boarding school, and there's a big chunk of my life when I didn't have my dad around so I could watch his actions as a spiritual leader. I don't have any memory of my dad leading family devotions or family prayer; I just remember him praying before meals. My dad is a godly man and a great example, but I just don't remember much spiritual leadership at home. He was a pastor as I am, and I learned from him how to pastor other people's families—just not my own.

   Find out how the father in your man's life lived. Men who grew up with fathers who read the Bible and prayed over every meal have a bigger foot in the door than men who grew up in homes that lacked a spiritual leader.
4. I sometimes feel spiritually inferior to Tina. Tina is one of those people who hasn't done too much wrong—at least on the surface. I've never heard her curse, and she's never smoked, drunk alcohol,

or cheated anyone. She is a real saint. I've often felt that Tina is the one who should be leading us spiritually—not because she's perfect, but because I sometimes feel she's just better than I am. Perhaps the man in your life feels you're more spiritual than he is, that you exude the glow of a saint. If so, there are ways you can set your man up for success when you recognize those moments.

Getting to the Heart of It

TINA 🌿 Before we get to the ways women can come alongside their messed up men, let's step back and peel away a few layers. Let's get to the heart of why, when the men in our life don't lead spiritually, it triggers an emotional response. Doing so can help us come to a greater understanding of our situation.

Think about this question before moving on: What drives my need to have the man in my life take up the role of spiritual leader in my home? Do I need him to lead spiritually because . . .

+ that's what I believe the Bible teaches?
+ women should submit to their husbands, and it's difficult to submit when he's not leading?
+ that's what I was taught?
+ our church teaches us that's how things should be done?
+ my children need spiritual leadership?
+ I want to see him grow in the Lord?
+ I need to grow and am looking for him to lead me?

My prayer is that all men will rise up and serve their families as spiritual leaders. However, we still need to evaluate why a man's lack of spiritual leadership so often becomes a sore spot in our hearts. By assessing our motives, we can better understand how to equip, encourage, and come alongside our messed up men as well as deal with the changes we might need to make in order to help them do so.

How did you answer the questions above? Do your reasons come from passed-down traditions, expectations you've gleaned from your church, a sincere desire to see the man in your life grow, or because you need him to fill a void in your life? If you answered anything other than wanting to see him grow in Christ, then more digging into your own heart and motives may be in order. Part of becoming the spiritual head of a home is growing in Christ.

My Battle . . . Your Battle?

My children were born around the time my husband began pastoring his first church full-time. I wanted him to do more as the spiritual leader of our home—and he was a pastor!

I tried getting my husband to fill a void in my own life, to meet a need. I would never say the word *need* around my counselor friend Tom; that's a no-no. Picture head shaking, index-finger wagging. Tom has taught me that *need* is a bad word; if we turn to others to fill voids and meet certain needs in our life, then we are not turning to the One who should be responsible for that. God is the only one who can fulfill every need we have.

But is it okay to desire a spiritually mature man? Of course it is—we all pray for that.

Here's my issue (and perhaps yours too): I wanted Dave to pray with our kids. I feared they would grow up, as I did, without spiritual leadership from their father. So I went overboard in my desire to have a spiritual leader in our home, and I tried to make it happen. My desire had a lot to do with my feeling left out of having a father as the spiritual leader of our home. I didn't want that for my children.

So I placed a great expectation upon Dave to perform and act a certain way as the spiritual leader. Ladies, I've had "the talk" with my husband too. You know, the one where you sit down and urge your man to step it up or he's in the doghouse.

But I held a twisted view. Because Dave didn't openly lay hands on our children every day and pray over them in front of me didn't mean he wasn't praying for them or teaching them how to pray. In fact, he probably prayed over our kids more than I did. I just didn't see him doing it. He prayed while he rocked them to sleep, during his morning quiet times, while they played, and when they were sick. That may be true for the man in your life as well, and also for the men who aren't fathers. Perhaps they are praying, just not in your view.

I wanted Dave to saturate our home with an abundance of spirituality. But really, what was that supposed to look like? Did he know? He didn't have a clue. I felt that because Dave was not only a Christian man but also a pastor, he didn't struggle like most men, didn't go through moments of needing to be fed or lacking the desire to pray, didn't sometimes put aside his Bible. I wanted him to drape a huge cape over his shoulders and fly around like Superman, scattering spiritual pixie dust all over the place. Sometimes I forgot he was just a simple man living in the world as all men do, in the flesh, and every day going through the process of trying to die to self.

I wanted Dave to be perfect in every way, displaying the fruit of the Spirit and walking around the house like Jesus. Wow—that's a tough one. He may have come close to looking like Jesus a few times when he slipped on leather sandals and grew his hair out, and there were moments when the fruit of the Spirit showered our home and saturated our family. But there were also moments of weakness, times that were dry and bleak. At some point, I concluded that Dave was a spiritual leader; his leadership just didn't look like I felt it should look.

The question is, who did God create your messed up man to be? We all agree we want the men in our life to grow and become strong men of God. But do we expect them to step into ginormous shoes and become perfect in leading out in a spiritual way? I hear some of you now, "Yes, I do!" God created us with different personalities, strengths, and qualities. None is better than the other, and it is helpful to recognize those qualities in the men in our life. Some men lead with a quiet spirit and by their actions, because that's how God created them. Then there are men who come out of the gate full speed ahead with outgoing personalities, are born leaders who rally the troops, and don't mind being the center of attention in their families.

I soon learned that each situation involving our children offered opportunity for both my husband and me to respond as spiritual leaders. There were moments when I stepped up as the spiritual leader, and there were times Dave led in ways I could never lead.

As a worship leader, I sang to my kids and taught them about worship. Dave taught them about Scripture and biblical history. In an informal way, our biblical discussions became teaching moments for our children. Kids hear everything.

I prayed through strongholds and sicknesses; Dave prayed through hardships and trials.

I took the kids to movies and related the movies to stories in the Bible, spiritual warfare, and conquering life's battles. I looked for ways to share the gospel with my kids and tried to use everyday moments to do it. Dave spoke about politics, God, and country. He shared Baptist history and told incredible stories. We both led in our own passionate ways. And even though our kids are grown now, we continue to lead in this way. The kids come to us both. They seem to know which one of us to go to for various issues in their lives.

Hope for the Almost

I'm one of those kids who grew up in a home without a Christian father. But though my father did not give his life to Christ until later on, that never stopped us from praying before meals, talking about sermons, or testifying about what God did in our lives. My mother became the spiritual leader of our home. On many occasions my siblings and I heard her shout, "Praise God! I prayed for that. God answered my prayer!" We openly discussed what God did in our lives, at church, or during the youth group.

My father missed the moments we kids walked down the aisle and gave our hearts to Christ. He missed our baptisms, church dinners, gospel sing-alongs, banquets, and youth events. He missed prayers before dinner—but there came a time, many years later, when he joined hands with us grown children and our families in a big circle, bowed his head, and prayed with us. That *almost there* moment caused our hearts to leap. Seeds were planted.

My dear friend, please do not give up hope. Continue to do everything you can to plant seeds and drop rose petals along the way. It may take a while, but the fruit of your labor will ripen throughout your home and push out the darkness. Everything you do that is of God, about God, and for God will be used by God. Stay on the right path. Don't harden your heart, but as Peter says, win the messed up man in your life over with your actions rather than your words.

My mother projected God's love, which in return allowed her to love a man like my dad. You have the ability to exude everything good and lovely that the Father gives you—and the messed up man in your life will see it.

Battling Boredom and Blues

Solomon is difficult to figure out. His story reminds me of smart kids in school who get bored because they're unchallenged. Sounds like one of my sons. After learning of some issues in school, I asked the school counselor to check in on him. This is what she observed:

The teacher gave instruction for the kids to take out their math papers and complete the sheet in thirty minutes. My son, instead of taking out his sheet, opened his bag of chips. (Glad I didn't see that; I would have gasped at the sight.) The counselor watched my son slowly consume each chip, one by one, without urgency. After eating the entire bag, he strolled over to the water fountain. About five minutes before it was time to turn in his paper, he reached down, without panic, and grabbed his math sheet. The counselor said he finished with a few strokes, walked up to the desk, and handed his sheet to the teacher. Her conclusion: "He's bored!"

Solomon had everything in the world: more wisdom than any other living person, more glory than any other king before him, and great exaltation before the Israelites by God. He was a deep thinker, a pas-sionate lover, and no doubt a handsome man. He was every girl's dream. So what happened?

The Bible says that "when Solomon was old, his wives turned his heart away after other gods." After all those years, did Solomon grow tired, bored, and unchallenged? Ecclesiastes gives us a clue into his mind-set as he questions the meaning of life and the reason for living. "'Meaningless! Meaningless!' says the Teacher. 'Utterly meaningless! Everything is meaningless'" (Eccl. 1:2 NIV). Everything looks and feels the same, day after day. Then Solomon adds, "Is there anything of which one can say, 'Look! This is something new?'" (v. 10 NIV).

Wisdom, pleasure, and toil were meaningless; Solomon hated his life and all the things he labored for under the sun, because he knew he had to leave them to the person who came after him (Eccl. 2:18). After achieving everything he ever wanted in life, it seems that Solomon just grew tired of it all.

When our lives become stagnant, flat, and unchallenged, we often fall away from our passions, work, and desire to grow. The same could be said of our spiritual walk. The Bible says that Solomon's heart was not wholly devoted to God. When did Solomon allow his devotion to slip through his fingers? When he grew old, tired, bored, or weary? Sometimes we tire of reading the Bible or going to church. Perhaps Solomon became tired of his daily routine and longed for something more. Instead of pressing deeper into God, he grew weary, disarmed himself, and gave into abdicating his position as the spiritual leader.

Most leaders know they need to stay on top of things in order to lead. That means reading, gathering information, going to training, studying, and equipping themselves. The same could be said of the messed up man we desire to lead our family. Here's a thought: do you see the man in your life reading, absorbing, studying, listening, equipping, yet according to you he still doesn't meet the qualifications of a spiritual leader? Maybe it's time to shift your thinking.

A Fresh Look

Right before his death, King David voiced a beautiful charge to his son Solomon. What a moment that must have been for this son getting ready to step into his father's shoes. Though David had messed up time and again, even as a father, he got this moment right.

"I am about to go the way of all the earth," he said. "So be strong, act like a man, and observe what the Lord your God requires: Walk in obedience to him, and keep his decrees and commands, his laws and regulations, as written in the Law of Moses. Do this so that you may prosper in all you do and wherever you go and that the Lord may keep his promise to me: 'If your descendants watch how they live, and if they walk faithfully before me with all their heart and soul, you will never fail to have a successor on the throne of Israel.'" (1 Kings 2:2–4 NIV)

Such wise words coming from a once failing father! As long as the man in your life is trying to keep God's laws, walk in obedience to Him, and observe His teachings, then he's probably doing a pretty good job. Breathe; it's okay. Come alongside your man and tell him he's doing great.

Well, what *does* a spiritual leader look like? Let's start with the obvious: if the man of the house does not know the Lord, he cannot lead spiritually. That said, let's look at the two words *spiritual* and *leader*. The *Oxford Dictionary* defines *spiritual* as "relating to, or affecting the human spirit or soul as opposed to material or physical things . . . or relating to religion or religious belief."[2] We understand the word *leader* is something or someone who leads.

Where debates arise on this matter is *how* someone is to lead. John Quincy Adams reputedly said, "If your actions inspire others to dream more, learn more, do more and become more, you are a leader."[3]

The Bible says a man is to lead in the following ways:

+ Submitting to Christ as his head (1 Cor. 11:3)
+ Being an imitator of Christ (Eph. 5:1)
+ Walking in love (1 Peter 1:22)
+ Keeping God's commandments (1 Kings 8:61)
+ Seeking instruction from his pastor or priest (Mal. 2:7)
+ Living with his wife in an understanding way (1 Peter 3:7)
+ Honoring his wife (1 Peter 3:7)
+ Not provoking his children to anger, but bringing them up in the discipline and instruction of the Lord (Eph. 6:4)

♦ Testifying of God's love and works among his children and household (Deut. 6:6–9)

To that, let's add King David's counsel "to be strong, act like a man, and observe what the Lord your God requires: Walk in obedience to him, and keep his decrees and commands, his laws and regulations."

Do you recognize any of those qualities in your messed up man? Perhaps he *is* leading, just not in the way you expect. If the man in your life holds Christ as the head, tries to imitate Christ, walks in love, seeks instruction, honors his wife, does not provoke his kids, and works hard to live with his wife in an understanding way, is he not leading by his actions and words? If you can see the fruits of the Spirit developing in his life, is he not leading by example?

We create our own perceptions of how leading is to look. Henry Cloud says, "In the end, as a leader, you are always going to get a combination of two things: what you create and what you allow."[4]

Five Ways to Encourage and Help Build a Strong Spiritual Leader

1. **Become a positive example.** Read, pray, and talk openly about God. He'll see, and pick up on the seeds you plant.

2. **Take note of "got it right" moments.** When you see him praying, reading the Bible, going to church, or attending a men's Bible study, affirm his actions.

3. **Set him up for success.** You start the devotions, take turns reading a Scripture or part of the Bible story, and praying. If the man in your life is sitting in on the devotion, then that's a praise moment!

4. **Boost his ego.** Encourage him to attend events for men or to get involved in a men's project by boosting his ego. He can add a lot by attending.

5. **Lower your expectations.** The more we expect of him, the more disappointed we will be if he doesn't meet those expectations. Allow God to work in his life and you be there to walk with him.

Moving Beyond the Mess

1. Everyone's view of what constitutes a spiritual leader is different. How would *you* define a spiritual leader?
2. What do you desire in men as spiritual leaders?
3. Do women sometimes place more focus on the man leading than growing? Consider Solomon and his circumstances. What are ways that a man can be a great leader and yet stagnate in his spiritual growth? Which would you consider more important in your family—for your man to do all the right things, or work toward becoming the right man? Why?
4. Look back over some of the characteristics Tina pulled out of Scripture that talk about how a man is to lead. Relate these to the men in your life. Do they display any of those characteristics? Explain.
5. *Moving to a healthier place:* Consider the "Five Ways to Encourage and Help Build a Strong Spiritual Leader." What other ideas might you add? While God is working on your man, what can you do to stay in a good place in mind, spirit, and heart rather than becoming bitter or frustrated? Read Romans 8:1–8.

May you be an encourager rather than a discourager. May you build up rather than tear down, instill hope not fear, and set your sight upon the change God can make in you and in the men in your life. May the Lord use you to plant seeds of leadership and affirm moments when the men in your life step toward God.

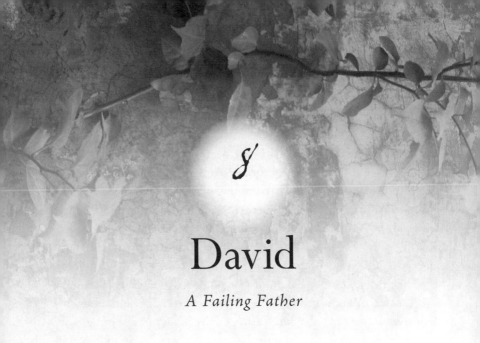

David

A Failing Father

Train up a child in the way he should go,
even when he is old he will not depart from it.
PROVERBS 22:6

Amnon rose from his bed, breathed deeply, and let out a long sigh. He was a man obsessed, burning with passion for his half sister Tamar.

"Why does the king's son look so haggard these days?" asked Jonadab, his adviser, entering the room.

"I'm in love with Tamar, my brother Absalom's sister."

"Ah, yes, Tamar," said Jonadab. "Here's what you do: Go to bed and pretend to be ill. When your father comes to see you, tell him you'd like Tamar to come prepare your meal and feed it to you by hand. Then when she does . . ."

Amnon took Jonadab's advice, David agreed to his son's request, and Tamar arrived and did the cooking. But instead of eating, Amnon cleared the house of everyone except Tamar. "Bring the food here into my bedroom so I can eat from your hand," he told her. The unsuspecting

Tamar complied, and that's when Amnon grabbed her. "Come to bed with me, my sister," he said.

Horrified, Tamar pled with her brother. "Don't force me! How could I ever get rid of my disgrace? And you—your character will be ruined." But there was no reasoning with the lust-crazed Amnon. What ensued is one of the uglier moments in the Bible, and rape was just part of Amnon's wickedness. Once he'd had his way with Tamar, his "love" for her flipped to an even more intense hatred. "Get out!" he yelled at her.

She protested. "Don't add evil to evil," she begged. But summoning his servant, Amnon had her thrown out and the door locked behind her. Tamar, devastated, poured ashes on her head, tore the ornate robe she wore as a virgin daughter of the king, and went away sobbing (see 2 Sam. 13:1–19).

Our hearts ache. We want to scoop up Tamar in our arms and wipe away her tears. We want to wash the ash from her head and restore her garment to perfection—the garment that symbolized her virginity. Amnon's crime makes our hearts boil. We want justice for Tamar.

We could spend the entire chapter delving into Amnon's messed up life. But let's dig deeper, beyond Amnon's awful sin to the heart of yet another messed up man: Amnon's father. By sifting through King David's life, perhaps we can understand why his son messed up so terribly. The story continues . . .

When Love Fails to Act

DAVE �֍ There David sits, up on the rooftop of his palace—an excellent spot for the musician-king to play his harp, calm his nerves, and clear his thoughts. David's fingers dance across the strings, and a prayer escapes his lips as a spontaneous song. His thoughts turn to his oldest son, who lies sick in bed. Just a short while ago, David had visited Amnon and offered the comfort only a father's presence can provide. David thinks of the day when he will share his kingdom with Amnon. Fathers have such dreams for their children—to pass on a legacy.

Suddenly the peaceful moment is interrupted by an urgent message

from his servant. "Pardon me, your majesty," the man says, nervously.
"Your daughter Tamar . . ."

A vague dread grips David. "Yes? What about her?"

"Tamar has been raped. By . . . by Amnon."

How does a dad respond to such news? What emotions charge
through David's heart? Shock? Confusion? Panic? In a single second,
all his hopes and dreams are cruelly crushed by the weight of a family
crisis. How will he handle this horrific situation?

He won't. "When King David heard of all these things, he became
very angry, but he would not punish his son Amnon, because he loved
him, for he was his firstborn" (2 Sam. 13:21 NRSV).

David's response to the rape of his daughter by his son was to do . . .
nothing.

Let's read it again. "He would not punish his son Amnon, because
he loved him."

Was that the reason? Was it love? Really? David avoided the problem, minimized the issue, and that was loving his son?

The truth is, love does not allow mistakes to go unchallenged. To the
contrary, the Bible instructs us to speak the truth in love (Eph. 4:15). To
speak the truth in love is to tell the truth, the whole truth, and nothing
but the truth. Speaking the truth in love tells the harsh reality of how
things really are. The "in love" part means that we speak the truth with an
understanding of the impact our words will have upon another. Speaking
the truth in love is not judgmental but restorative. Its goal is not to confront and condemn but to reveal and restore. If David let such a moment
like this slip, how many more teachable moments involving his children
did he allow to slide by? What would life have looked like if David had
stepped into fatherhood and addressed critical issues with his children?
Perhaps Amnon would have looked upon his sister in a different light.

A Messed Up Dad

Some aspects of King David's childhood are hard not to notice. Perhaps these experiences contributed to David's fathering issues. David
was indeed a messed up man, and often messed up men produce messed

up kids. I'm not blaming Amnon's behavior on David; however, David's lack of discipline toward his son may have added to Amnon's messed up life.

The prophet Samuel arrived in the small town of Bethlehem with the specific purpose of anointing Israel's next king. God told Samuel that one of Jesse's sons would be the king. First Samuel 16 describes the process Samuel undertook:

> When [Jesse and his sons] arrived, Samuel took one look at Eliab and thought, "Surely this is the Lord's anointed!"
>
> But the Lord said to Samuel, "Don't judge by his appearance or height, for I have rejected him. The Lord doesn't see things the way you see them. People judge by outward appearance, but the Lord looks at the heart." (vv. 6–7 NLT)

Jesse went through the trouble of presenting each of his sons to Samuel, but each time the Lord rejected them. Samuel finally asked, "Are these all the sons you have?'" No, Jesse said, his youngest son was out tending the flock.

> So Jesse sent for him. He was dark and handsome, with beautiful eyes.
>
> And the Lord said, "This is the one; anoint him."
>
> So as David stood there among his brothers, Samuel took the flask of olive oil he had brought and anointed David with the oil. And the Spirit of the Lord came powerfully upon David from that day on. (vv. 12–13 NLT)

I am struck by the fact that Jesse left David out of the gathering of his sons. To make matters worse, the text says that "all seven of Jesse's sons were presented to Samuel" (v. 10 NLT). David, the eighth son, was not included. It's as if he did not exist. Such self-identifying experiences are branded into a young man's identity: "I don't matter. I'm not important. I'm not useful. I don't count."

Why would Jesse not include his youngest son? Why deny David existed as a son? An out-of-the-box answer occurred to me a few years ago: What if David was illegitimate? What if he wasn't really Jesse's son? Or perhaps Jesse felt embarrassed about some aspect of David's birth. Maybe his conception was the result of an affair or some other less-than-holy experience. David himself makes a startling statement in Psalm 51: "Behold, I was brought forth in iniquity, and in sin my mother conceived me" (v. 5). What sin?

Let me add one more piece of speculative evidence. David chose to describe God as "a father of the fatherless" (Ps. 68:5). Whatever circumstances surrounded his birth, David must have carried some scars from his childhood in regard to his own father. If David was left out of such an important event as Samuel's invitation to Jesse and his sons, what other, less significant events might he also have been excluded from?

Immediately following David's anointing by Samuel, the Bible says David was chosen to play the harp for King Saul and to become his armor bearer. As a young man, David left home to take his first job working for the king. The Bible describes David at this point in his life as a talented harp player, a valorous warrior, and possessing good judgment. "He is a fine-looking young man," one of Saul's servants tells Saul, "and the Lord is with him." Up to this point in his young life, David had been a shepherd and thus spent large portions of his life in the wilderness caring for the sheep, defending them from predators, and passing the time by playing his instruments. He had the perfect resume for his new job.

How did David's move to the palace impact his relationship with his father? Did his dad even care? Did he miss David? Did King Saul take the young man under his wing? How much time did they spend together, and did Saul assume a fatherly role in David's life, at least in David's eyes? If not, then another fatherly figure has failed David in his short life.

By the time we get to 1 Samuel 18, we find David in a new role as a son-in-law to the king, best friends with the king's son, and the target of Saul's jealousy. For the rest of 1 Samuel, David is on the run as Saul tries to kill him. When David finally takes the throne of Israel, he has become a fearless warrior, a legendary leader—and a lousy dad.

Scripture is silent as to David's fathering skills in these early days of his kingdom. Perhaps I'm reading myself into David's narrative. I remember my first church as a full-time pastor. I was a young thirty-something, ambitious, and arrogant leader. I poured myself into my new role, attended classes at the nearby seminary, and gave whatever scraps of time I had left to my young family at home. I was a lousy dad in those early days of ministry. I imagine David similarly engrossed in his new kingly role, while his family is left at home to adjust on their own.

TINA ✖ I stood for the first time to speak in public. As a young college student perched behind the wooden podium in a small church, I felt terrified and my knees trembled. The goal was to share my testimony, but after a few words, something else pushed through: stored-up pain and long-suppressed tears of grief. Though I tried to control my emotions, the dam broke, and years of turmoil surfaced. An aching, cathartic cleansing took place at that moment.

And then, a tiny, hunchbacked woman shuffled toward the altar, thrust her hand upward, and waved a tissue at me as if waving a white flag. I reached down and clutched it, thanking her with my eyes. That moment became a day of surrender for me. There at the altar I confessed to a crowd of people, for the very first time, that I had a messed up father in need of help. And something else spilled out as well—my realization that I too needed healing.

At the very mention of the word *father*, many hearts shudder and shut down. Because—let's say it—fathers mess up. Messed up fathers often teach their children what their own messed up fathers taught them. And when children get their image of fathering from a messed up dad, then the messed up legacy can continue from one generation to another.

I can't conceive the depth of Tamar's pain after being raped and then watching her father do nothing. How did that affect Tamar's ability to love her dad? The severity of the impact caused her to leave her father's house and go live in her brother Absalom's house.

If I gave each of you a sheet of paper and asked you to list the characteristics of your messed up dad, our lists might align, but more than likely they would look different. Why? Because we each look at our fathers through unique lenses, needs, expectations, experiences, and childhood wounds. How do we love dads who mess up? There is hope. Below are three steps to take toward loving your father.

Step One: Love God First

God became my Father. I couldn't love my dad the way I wanted to until I allowed God to become my Father. It can be difficult to see God as a Father because of the wounding from our earthly father, but the truth is, I needed a dad, and God was a good place to start. God represented a father who would never hurt me—I trusted that. I learned that through Christ I could love my father, not out of my own ability but with God's help.

Step Two: Release the Responsibility

My friend and therapist, Michelle, puts it this way:

> As adults, generally we are able to come to an understanding that we are not the sole reason for things being the way they are; however, a difficult childhood is likely to skew our view. When we are ready to unburden ourselves of the responsibility for our messed up dad, it will require a fundamental shift in our thinking. We will have to move from owning all the responsibility to giving that ownership over to our dad. Each individual is 100 percent responsible for their own thoughts, feelings, and actions, regardless of the circumstances. Once we are able to know this, and then believe it, moving toward empathy and forgiveness becomes easier and the possibility of repairing the relationship seems possible, if not desirable.[1]

Step Three: Invest

I recognized that I needed to understand more of my dad's life. I wanted to know about my father, grandfather, and those before him. I guess you could say I chose to invest in my father. Did I have to? Of course not, but choosing to do nothing would have kept us distant. I became a detective and asked a lot of questions. As my knowledge of my father grew, my carefully crafted walls began to crumble at my feet.

My father understood about living with an alcoholic because his own father drank. He understood abandonment, poverty, and lack of nurturing. My father's past brought a greater clarity to why my father messed up so much. I empathized with the man who gave me reason to be angry. He too had suffered a life of living with a messed up dad. How could he have known any better? Empathizing with my father's childhood pain softened the parts of my heart I had hardened.

Years passed. It would have been easy to lose hope, but I began to see changes. My father came to know Christ, stopped drinking, and started life over. I watched as he clasped his grandchildren's tiny fingers and led them out to pick wild blackberries. I watched as he loaded fishing poles in the back of his truck, drove grandchildren to secret fishing holes, and shared lessons on baiting hooks. Afternoon golf cart rides, trips to the nearby convenience store for orange Push-Ups, and whisking sweet chocolate in cold milk were just a few of his grandfatherly activities. He teased, tickled, and treasured the kids. *Who is this man?* I wondered, watching from a distance. A still, peaceful voice answered, "He's your father."

My precious friends, may it be so in your own dad's life. Getting to know how he was fathered and empathizing with his pain doesn't excuse his behavior, but exploring his childhood may be the start of restoring your relationship with him. Every journey has a first step. Just remember, you never step alone—God steps with you.

Married to a Messed Up Man

To this day I haven't met a man who wasn't messed up in some way or another. Those men who try real hard to keep their lives looking clean and neat often fool themselves into thinking they have it all together. Ladies, we're in the same boat. We all have something in our lives we need to work on. It is inevitable that messed up women marry messed up men and messed up men marry messed up women. The hardship comes when men and women finally figure out the other is messed up. Perhaps the bliss of our wedding day blindsides us to our spouse's human side. As a starry-eyed young wife, I was shell-shocked the first time my husband fell off the pedestal on which I had placed him.

Once I began focusing on my husband's messes, my view of him changed. Of course it did; I was looking at the mess rather than the person behind the mess. Someone once said to me, "He's a great guy with a problem. Now what?" Wise words! I allowed the problem to crowd out the fact that Dave really was a wonderful person and he probably said the same of me. His good qualities and everything I fell in love with were still there.

Like me, you may be married to a great man who has issues. It's not the end of the world. God is the great mess manager, and He can clean up our messed up men far better than you or I can.

After years of ministering to women, I've come to the firm conviction that we are often just as messed up as the men in our lives—and maybe even more so. We often don't want to admit it, and blame our mess on our man. After all, it's easy to take our eyes off our own messed up life when someone else's mess is dangling in front of us.

Women wounded by messed up dads often misplace their focus. The perfect father they picture for their kids is the opposite of the dysfunction they lived with growing up. But if you grew up with a messed up dad, then your view of what a good father looks like may be skewed. Your childhood wounds and the way you were raised can affect your marriage, your parenting style (and how you view your mate's parenting style), and most importantly, your values.

I had a clear picture of what I *didn't* want in a father but not of what I *did* want. My lack of clarity created a swirl of emotions in my mind about how my husband should perform as a father. Did you catch that word, *perform*? I eventually learned how unhealthy that word is, both in my personal life and in my relationship with my spouse. My husband's purpose in life isn't to "perform" for me. Yet often we impose performance standards on our husbands because of the ways our fathers let us down.

Door-Busting Dads

My husband entered the house like Superman after a long day of work. He'd bust open the door, thrust his chest out, flex his pecs, and shout, "Daddy's home!" There I stood, stringy-haired, crinkled clothes, and smelling like baby powder (among other things).

Everyone landed on all fours, tables and chairs got shoved back, and the roughhousing started. Bawls, cries, growls, and groans filled the house like in a Godzilla movie. Boys raced through rooms and bounced off furniture. Small bodies sailed through the testosterone-charged air. Nothing stopped the frenzy. Well, almost nothing . . .

One evening, on his return trip to Earth from being tossed in the air by Daddy, a little one launched a stream of spit up at the center of Dave's chest. This wouldn't have phased some dads, but as for my husband, well—let's just say Superman came face to face with his kryptonite. Grimacing, the Man of Steel raced to the bathroom. Little eyes stared in disbelief. "What's wrong with Daddy?"

Yes—what's wrong with Daddy? Some dads would have wiped it off, or not, and continued the adventure. Every woman wants her man to be a hero, but sometimes it doesn't take much to bring a man to his knees. We see it, our kids see it, and God sees it. Kids look upon their dads as giant champions, and women sometimes expect it of their men as well. Have we forgotten that we're all flawed?

Perhaps your husband isn't the door-busting dad you want for your kids. Maybe he avoids or minimizes issues, isn't the spiritual leader you desire, has a difficult time speaking into your child's life, doesn't take action, and appears checked out. In other words, he's a lot like King David.

David's refusal to confront Amnon is difficult to understand. I can't imagine how Maacah, Tamar's mother, felt about it. Clutching her distraught daughter must have been overwhelming in itself, but then for her husband to do absolutely nothing to reprove Amnon for the pain he had caused his sister—well, that must have been a grief beyond comprehension.

My friend Michelle says, "This is the place where speaking the truth in love becomes the duty of the women who love their messed up men, so that they can learn to be accountable, so positive, healthy behaviors can replace hurtful ones, and relationships can be healed and restored."[2] In Maacah's case, such truth-telling may have been much harder than today; in biblical times, addressing the king was difficult in itself. Nevertheless, we get a clear picture of a messed up father who needs help, healing, and restoration.

Famed as he was for his valor in battle, why could David not find the courage to approach his son? The Scripture says that when David received the news, he was furious. If he was that angry, what kept him from reproaching Amnon? Was love really the reason he chose not to address his son? Or might David's shame over his own indiscretion with Bathsheba have rendered him silent? For whatever reason, David more than likely had no idea how to bust through the door and step out as a dad. So he did nothing.

If we can recognize similar moments in our own messed up man, perhaps we'll choose different words and a different way of approaching him.

Imparting Courage

Consider the word *discourage*. Its prefix, *dis-*, involves the removal or opposition of something—in this case, courage. To discourage means to remove or weaken courage in a person. But that's not all: *dis* has taken on a life of its own as a slang verb. Derived from the word *disrespect*, *dis* can mean "belittle," "criticize," or "cut down to size."

Who knew that three small letters could change a person's life? That they could make a person feel weak and scared?

But what happens if we rip away the first three letters from *discourage*? Then the word becomes *courage*. In order to instill courage in another person, we must *encourage* him or her. Author William Arthur Ward is credited with the following wisdom: "Flatter me, and I may not believe you. Criticize me, and I may not like you. Ignore me, and I may not forgive you. Encourage me, and I will not forget you. Love me, and I may be forced to love you."

Encourage. This powerful French-derived word dates back to the fifteenth century, and its meaning, "to inspire with courage, spirit, or hope,"[3] resonates with us today. It means to strengthen the heart. When we encourage, we fortify the heart of another person.

I confess I do not use my words to encourage my husband as much as I should. More times than I want to admit, I have allowed praiseworthy moments to slip through my fingers. But I want to get better at it, don't you? So how can we instill courage in the men we love? One way is to set them up for success.

The book *Brothers!* puts it this way:

> The word *encourage* comes from the same word as one of the names of the Holy Spirit. It is a word meaning "called alongside to help." To encourage one another, then, is to be vitally involved in what the Spirit is doing in the lives of our brothers in Christ. Either verbally or through our actions, we can affirm God's view of our brothers. In doing so, we move from accepting them to helping them in some tangible way. Encouragement is taking an active role in a brother's life.[4]

When we encourage, we give courage. When we give courage, we strengthen the heart. How does God tell us to strengthen the heart?

Commission. In Deuteronomy 3:28, God tells Moses to commission Joshua, to "charge Joshua and encourage him." The word charge in Hebrew means to command—give orders. God wants Moses to give Joshua the courage to follow through with his task, to spur Joshua on, to help him become strong. We women can do the same thing when it comes to setting up our men for success. Let's become his biggest cheerleader.

How to Set Up Men for Success

Boast when they get it right.

Equip them with the necessary tools to succeed.

Express what daughters need from their fathers.

Allow personal days for refueling.

Encourage adventurous "man days" with their sons.

Speak kindly. In 2 Samuel 19:7, when Joab tells David to go out and encourage his men, the Hebrew means "to speak kindly" to them. The flow of gentle words can impart courage.

Strengthen. We see in 1 Thessalonians 5:14 that we are to "encourage the fainthearted, help the weak, be patient with everyone." The Greek word translated as "encourage" means to speak to, calm, and console. Our strength in patience can become his strength in life.

God's desire is for men to succeed, and we women can help them do so by encouraging them.

The Blessing

"It's not about you." Words like those are tough to swallow, especially if we feel connected to the situation. Ladies, here it is: you can't fix your messed up man! Furthermore, your messed up man can't even fix himself. He is the product of years of living, years of experiences, and years of succeeding and failing. My husband says, "Men are a compilation of every experience and relationship they have ever lived through. Some experiences have bettered your man while others have battered him. The man standing before you is the result of a lifetime of surviving."

That said, I'm not saying you should do nothing, just sit by and watch the train wreck. There is something you can and ought to do—something much more difficult than the extremes of either fixing or doing nothing.

The greatest example of fathering comes from God our Father. His Word teaches, corrects, and directs in the way we should live, and that applies to our men in their roles as fathers. When we drape His character around us like a cloak, we receive incredible strength and character from God the Father, who shapes us into the most amazing people. And therein lies the secret. When you place the cloak of the Father's character around your messed up man, he will begin to be shaped by the form of the coat—the form of the Father's character. You don't fix him—God does. Your role is to dress him in the Father's clothing by blessing him with your words, your countenance, and your touch.

A few years ago, a friend gave my husband a book that focuses on the topic of the Old Testament ritual of blessing.[5] My husband was a successful pastor living without his father's blessing and not aware that he needed it. In the Old Testament, fathers often laid their hands upon their sons and spoke a blessing into their life. My husband spent much of his life searching for his father's blessing. Without his father's blessing, it was difficult for my husband to bless our own two sons. Blessing the man in your life helps build the cloak of the Father's character that you want to place around him.

A blessing has three dimensions that I encourage you to adopt if you want to dress your man in the character of fatherhood.

1. Bless with Your Words

Our words are powerful forces. The book of James equates our words with the rudder on a ship, a bit in a horse's mouth, and even a spark that starts a roaring fire (James 3:3–6). Our words have enough power to turn the men in our lives, and others we care about, in a variety of directions. Through words of blessing, we can steer our messed up men forward to a glorious present and future. First Peter 4:11 says, "If anyone speaks, they should do so as one who speaks the very words of God" (NIV). How does God see the man in your life? What would He say to him? When your messed up man looks like a father—let him know. Speak it into his life! Resist criticism and relish character building.

2. Bless with Your Expressions

Let your facial expressions bless. What our looks communicate often has much more power than what we say. Job reflects on days before his suffering; days his presence and character blessed others. He says, "They waited for me as for showers and drank in my words as the spring rain. When I smiled at them, they scarcely believed it; the light of my face was precious to them" (Job 29:23–24 NIV). Wow—to have moments like that where our smiles and facial expressions bless others.

3. Bless with Your Hands

A final way to bless is with your hands. Like words, an expression of approval given through a simple pat on the back or a hug contains immense blessing. Like a facial expression, a well-timed touch can communicate emotions much more deeply than words. A touch communicates strength, security, acceptance, affirmation, and lasting love. Jesus set this example for us: "He took them in His arms and began blessing them, laying His hands on them" (Mark 10:16).

Three Ways to Bless

1. With your words (1 Peter 4:11)
2. With your expressions (Job 29:23–24)
3. With your hands (Mark 10:16)

A few years back, my father-in-law, eighty at the time, came to visit. During the Sunday morning service, my husband asked his dad (a retired pastor) if he would be willing to bless his grandsons. He agreed. My husband invited his father to come sit in a chair at the front of the worship center. He explained to the congregation that he had asked his dad to bless our sons in the Old Testament tradition by laying hands on their heads and speaking a blessing into their lives.

My sons came and knelt before their grandfather. My father-in-law placed his trembling and weathered hands upon their heads. He prayed and spoke blessings into their young lives. It was quite an emotional experience, one I doubt my sons will ever forget. At the end, my husband approached his dad to help lift him from his chair. But his father said, "David, I'm not done." He pulled my husband to his knees, put his hand on his head, and began to speak blessing into his life—the blessing my husband wanted so much, yet never thought to ask for.

That picture is the perfect image of what God wants to do, not only to messed up men but to men all over the world. Our heavenly Father wants to pull them to their knees and declare, "I'm not done!" He wants to speak bold blessings into their lives. He wants to pull out the garbage and shine up the armor. He wants to affirm destiny, purpose, and freedom! And when all is said that needs to be said, God desires to take His strong arms and lift each newfound man to his feet.

As women, may we continue to pray and seek such a moment—for in the end, not just our man but we too will come away with a greater understanding of courage, strength, and blessing.

Moving Beyond the Mess

1. Consider David and the incident with Amnon. Why do you suppose it was difficult for David to address the issue with his son? Can you relate your answer to your own family dynamics? What do you think were the eventual repercussions of David's failure to confront Amnon?

2. Reflect on your upbringing. Was there a man in your life who helped raise you? If so, share about his parenting abilities.

3. How would a man's upbringing affect his parenting abilities?

4. Which of the three forms of blessing—blessing with your words, your expressions, or your hands—do you find it hardest to practice with the men in your life? Why?

5. Tina wrote about how Dave's father blessed his grandsons and Dave himself. Take a look at another man who blessed his sons in Genesis 27:27–29. Though Jacob deceived Isaac, Isaac's blessing

nevertheless remained upon Jacob. Which part of that blessing stands out to you? What did Isaac pray would happen to those who blessed his son?

6. *Moving to a healthier place:* Read 1 John 3:1. How does this help you see the men in your life? What do you think God will do for us when we bless the men in our life?

---

*May God give you the courage to encourage, and may
He pour His blessings on those you bless with your words,
expressions, and hands. And may God bless you with
abundant love for the men in your life.*

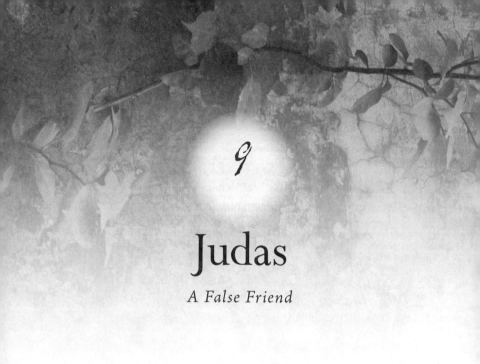

9

Judas

A False Friend

Accountability breeds response-ability.
STEPHEN R. COVEY, *PRINCIPLE-CENTERED LEADERSHIP*

Thunderous laughter erupted from around the rustic table, inviting others to join the circle. Men reached across one another for helpings of fresh bread, fruit, meat, and wine. It was a boisterous group gathered to enjoy conversation, stories, and the presence of one man who had captured the attention of so many. There were tax collectors, sinners, and disciples—and Jesus. It was a study of contrasts, of dark and light, meshed together to create a masterpiece; a moment of fellowship between men investing in one another.

"Why is your Teacher eating with the tax collectors and sinners?" the Pharisees asked Jesus's disciples. Jesus overheard. "It is not those who are healthy who need a physician, but those who are sick," He told them.

In that moment a bond was forged between brothers—brothers with difficulties, sinful natures, and fleshly behaviors. Men who sometimes messed up and got it wrong. Brothers of every stripe walking with each other and embracing the teachings of a man who appeared to be just like them.

Who was this Jesus who welcomed such men into His presence? This Jesus who seemed not only to understand hearts and souls but to seek them out, broken, scarred, and tainted as they were?

Many men wondered. Among them, reclining, eating, and laughing with the rest, was Judas. Did he question, "Who is this Jesus? The one people pin their hopes and future on? The one others fall at the feet of, grab hold of, and follow after?"

Did walking with Jesus cause Judas to question himself, "Who am I? What am I doing with a man like this?"

Disciple of Christ

DAVE ✳ I haven't always seen the value in having good friends. In fact, I'm not sure I've been a very good friend for most of my life. It's always been difficult for me; I guess I have some tendencies to be introverted. I prefer time by myself over groups. Hanging out with people seems like a lot of work to me. Yet during those moments of meeting with friends, I often come away feeling refreshed, restored, and loved.

Somewhere along the way, I taught myself that people can't be trusted. If people find out who I really am, what I think, value, and enjoy, they will eventually reject me. Believing that has made it a lot easier to keep to myself. I'm grateful to God that by going through some very difficult times, I learned what it means to have trusted friends who walk with me. And I've been able to be such a friend myself.

I've always been told that men need other men with whom to share their lives. Previously I gave mental assent to the idea, but over the past decade I have come to understand its truth in my heart. I need men in my life who tell me the truth about myself and others. I need men who are not afraid to honestly share their lives, successes, and struggles. I need men near me with whom I can share accountability.

Judas is known throughout history as the man who betrayed Jesus. You know the story. He sold Jesus into enemy hands for thirty pieces of silver. Judas led the group that arrested Jesus, using the sign of a brotherly kiss to identify their target. Later he regretted his decision and tried to give the money back. His tragic story ends in suicide.

Describing Judas requires us first to recognize that he was chosen by Jesus. Judas didn't accidentally join the team. Jesus handpicked Judas, as he did the other eleven, to come and follow him as a disciple. Judas was given a particular assignment as treasurer (John 12:6), most likely because he was the most trusted of the disciples. When picking a treasurer, we look for someone we all trust; I imagine the disciples looked for the same quality and would have approved of the choice. But Judas was not trustworthy. He would occasionally take a little off the top for his own expenses.

Who was this Judas? Why did he need money? Or was his true character simply that of a thief?

Judas may have been a zealot—a militant looking to overthrow the Roman government by whatever means necessary. Only Jesus would pick zealots and tax collectors to serve on the same team. Tax collectors were doing the dirty work for the Romans—collecting high taxes from the people and enjoying a good living in return. Matthew and Judas would have been natural enemies. Yet Jesus brought them together to bring the gospel to the world.

Luke 9:1–2 says of Jesus, "He called the twelve together, and gave them power and authority over all the demons and to heal diseases. And He sent them out to proclaim the kingdom of God and to perform healing." Have you ever considered that Judas was able to heal the sick and cast out demons? We're so prone to demonize Judas that we forget he was with the other disciples, participating in all they did and experiencing everything they experienced. He was in the boat when Jesus walked on water and calmed the storm. Judas passed out miracle bread and fish to the five thousand. Judas saw and experienced the power and authority of Jesus.

So why would Judas in particular betray Jesus? Scholars have wrestled with the question and come up with various answers. One is that Judas betrayed Jesus because of disillusionment. Judas was a zealot who believed that Jesus would eventually, as Messiah, overthrow Roman tyranny and establish God's kingdom on earth. But as time went by, Jesus began to speak not of His earthly kingdom but of His heavenly kingdom, and of not destroying one's enemies but forgiving them, and of His approaching death. It wasn't the message Judas was hoping for. He ceased to believe in Jesus's mission and, consequently, in Jesus. Judas betrayed Him out of frustration and anger because Jesus was not using His popularity to build political power.

Another possibility is that Judas was financially desperate. His habit of stealing from the treasury he was tasked with managing is suggestive. Perhaps he needed cash fast, and betrayal offered a way to make some big money quickly.

Whatever Judas's reason, it strikes me as odd that nobody except Jesus knew that Judas was plotting to betray Jesus. After all, the disciples had forged a deep bond as they traveled together during the three short years of Jesus's ministry. They must have shared some amazing conversations. They discussed the meanings of the parables, argued over who was the greatest among them, and pondered the significance of the miraculous. I'm sure they debated religion, politics, and all the other things that concern us today. And they journeyed through hardships, toil, emotional discord, grumbling people, and violent crowds. Leaving houses and families which had given them a sense of community and fellowship, they cast their lot together with Jesus.

So I find it almost unbelievable that Judas would consider betraying Jesus without talking about it with at least one of the other disciples. What about Simon the Zealot? Surely he would have understood where Judas was coming from. And yet it appears that none of the disciples had any clue that Judas was on the path to betrayal.

On the night He was betrayed, Jesus became "troubled in spirit, and testified and said, 'Truly, truly, I say to you, that one of you will betray Me.' The disciples began looking at one another, at a loss to know of which one He was speaking" (John 13:21–22). No one had any idea that Judas had sold Jesus out. Judas was alone and isolated.

A Man's Isolation

At times, I've felt alone and isolated. And I've made some catastrophic decisions because I wasn't sharing my thoughts and life with trusted friends. Here's a quick example.

A few years back, I ran out of gas on my way to church. That's not entirely unusual, because I like to stretch a tank of gas as far as possible. As I realized the car was about to die, I used its final running moments to get off the main street and coast to the back corner of a parking lot. I did that because I was embarrassed for anyone to know I had run out of gas. And on Sunday of all things! Imagine the pastor sitting on the side of the road on his way to Sunday service. Coming from a small town, no doubt I would have been the topic of the day.

In my mind, running out of gas demonstrated I was irresponsible, foolish, and a poor manager of my money and possessions. I wanted to hide my car, conceal my predicament, and seek to somehow solve my problem without the help of others. I called my son and had him bring me some gas, which I quickly put in the car, hoping no one would see me.

If you're saying, "That's crazy!" then I agree. The truth is that I had many people in my life who would have gladly come to my side and assisted me without casting any judgment. In fact, if I had allowed it, I probably could have been picked up by a few church members on their way to church. But I didn't want to let anyone know I was a human being capable of mistakes, the least of which was running out of gas. Really—how many of us have run out of gas!

I suspect Judas didn't want anyone to know his tank was empty. He was a highly regarded disciple of Jesus the Messiah, and I suspect he couldn't stand the thought that someone might find out he was actually a thief and a betrayer. Though he shared a common bond, a common life, and a common calling with the other disciples, Judas withheld his struggle and shared it with no one.

Isn't it true that we sometimes open the paper only to discover that some celebrity, politician, or high-profile leader has fallen because their big secret has been exposed? It happens. Friends, coworkers, leaders at church can all let us down and betray us. I've heard men become brutally honest about their mistakes, their lapses in judgment, and their sin following a great fall. It would be so much better and easier if they could be honest *before* their world collapses around them. The hard part is the fall; although painful, sharing is easier. But most men choose isolation until the fall.

Judas, a man who could heal the sick and cast out demons, couldn't cast out his own demons in the end. None of us can. Men need other men who can speak the truth in love. Webster defines *accountable* as "subject to giving an account: answerable."[1] Accountability means that a man can be required to tell his story. Men, all men, need someone in their lives to whom they can tell their story. Accountability isn't about punishment, and it's not about allowing one's privacy to be abused. Accountability is about having someone in your life whom you trust enough to tell your story to—the whole story: the good, the bad, and the ugly. Accountability means a man's story counts!

As I'm writing, I'm thinking of three very good friends, men with whom I can share my story. These men know everything about my life—everything! They know all about my mistakes, my failures, my fears, and my dreams. I can share anything with these guys without having to worry about disclosure, dismissal, or derogatory comments. They love me!

There is a New Testament model for this kind of accountability. We see the apostle Paul being watched and encouraged by a man named Barnabas. Barnabas knew that Paul's story needed to be told, needed to count. And Barnabas made sure it happened.

In the same way, Paul took a young man named Timothy to his side and spoke life into him. Paul made sure that Timothy's story counted. Men need men! Men need men who can make sure their life story counts and is not wasted in regret and shame.

TINA ✗ As women, we understand the importance of friend-ships. We are like bright piñatas filled with information, stories, and data. Our babbling, chatter, and laughter burst into colorful hues of reds, pinks, and lavenders. Without the proper release we might burst. While men may not have the same need for outlets as women, we realize men do need the fellowship of other men.

Though Judas walked with other disciples in a close-knit community, he also walked alone. I feel sad about that. Did Judas feel it wasn't safe to trust these men with his inner struggle? Did he feel embarrassed to confess his thoughts and temptations? Was he afraid the disciples might get angry, throw him out of the group, or disown him? Could confessing to a friend or having another man hold him accountable have kept him from betraying Jesus or stealing money from the ministry's purse? And who were the women in his life? There is no record of Judas ever marrying, but we know he had a mother. I can't imagine how she felt about losing her son.

Is it any different in today's world? We hear the news of tragic school shootings. Teens shoot peers they went to class with, walked with, ate with, played sports with, had conversations with, and attended school events with. One teen shoots other teens and then himself, and his mother faces the double grief of her child's murderous actions and his own suicide. And the tragedy isn't limited to impulsive kids. Grown men walk into a business, shoot their coworkers, and then turn the gun on themselves. Their family's shock and grief are unbearable. Such can be the costly ripple effect of isolation and aloneness, of not being known in places where a man most deeply needs to be known.

How is it that men can walk with those closest to them and yet still feel alone? Not that the problem is limited to men; women can be just as prone to it. Have you been there? Have you walked among crowds and still felt isolated and secluded? Do you hold on to zealously guarded secrets, deep emotions, and turmoil, never allowing the shadows to surface?

I grew up with eight brothers with different personalities, likes, dislikes, and ways of handling things. Some of my brothers had no problem confessing details of their lives; others kept to themselves. We have both kinds of men in our lives. How can we help a man bring the painful stuff of his inner world into the light, where he can experience acceptance and support rather than isolation and aloneness? That's where accountability enters the picture.

Accountability 101

There are different approaches to accountability, some healthy and helpful, others unhealthy and counterproductive.

I love what Beth Moore said: "Men are not our problem; it's what we are trying to get from them that messes us up. Nothing is more baffling than our attempt to derive our womanhood from our men. We use guys like mirrors to see if we're valuable. Beautiful. Desirable. Worthy of notice. Viable."[2]

A woman's insecurities often push her toward trying to keep the men in her life accountable. I have to ask, because I'm guilty of it myself, do you require the man in your life to explain his actions or decisions, where he's been, what he's been up to? Women do that for various reasons.

I'm reminded of those times when I've left the house for a "me" day. Upon my return, Dave greets me with smiles and hugs. The first thing out of his mouth is, "Did you have fun?" How different from what I sometimes greet him with: "Where have you been?" He always shares, but how do I get past trying to keep him accountable?

Women often feel it's their role to keep the messed up men in their life accountable. That sometimes comes with a big stick and a stern look. Some women feel accountability gives them the right to check a man's Facebook account, cell phone, emails, coat pockets, and underwear drawers. (We won't talk about women who dig through trash. If you're one of those—keep reading.) Anything—searching for anything that might give them the right to stand up and shout, "Aha! I knew you were up to something!"

Women can become consumed with trying to unravel what they believe are well-kept secrets, failures, and troubles. This wasted energy puts a toll on our physical and emotional well-being. It strains fingers from searching the Internet and calluses knees from digging through trash, laundry, and beneath beds. It overloads our senses and thoughts. Spying and listening in on phone conversations doesn't help. A counselor would say such behavior is futile and leads men to find creative evasions. However, if you're working with a counselor on reestablishing trust or confidence in your relationship, please be diligent in working as he or she suggests.

There are various forms of accountability.

Personal. Accountability to oneself is tough because it requires a big dose of self-discipline (something I struggle with). Women understand this when trying to set healthy schedules, goals, and boundaries, lose weight, change habits, and so on. This kind of accountability can involve spiritual growth as we make ourselves accountable to God. Of course our accountability to God should be first and foremost. Without God's help in our accountability, personal accountability can be difficult to achieve.

Accountability with friends. Friends sometimes keep each other accountable. A text at the end of the day says, "No carbs today (thumbs up)." A friend sits with another friend, surrounded by a mound of tissues, and says, "Are you ready to get help?" We need friends like that, who tell us we're blowing it, getting into trouble with this man, losing control of our life; friends who will pull us away from bad crowds. We need friends who speak the truth, and we need to understand that when they do, it comes from a deep, burning love for us. We need friends like Jesus who walked with a group of dysfunctional men, taught them His ways, and kept them accountable.

But there is another kind of accountability women must understand, and that is the kind of accountability men need.

Accountability for Men

Below are three things in particular that women need to know about accountability for men.

1. It's not about you. Though we want to be our man's best friend, and some of us may already fill that spot, his issue with accountability is not about our keeping him on the right track or being his best buddy. Men need men. A woman becoming a man's accountability partner potentially puts the woman in an unhealthy role over the man.

2. *A good accountability partner starts with a good connection.* The Bible teaches that "two are better than one because they have a good return for their labor. For if either of them falls, the one will lift up his companion. But woe to the one who falls when there is not another to lift him up" (Eccl. 4:9–10). We saw this with Judas. His choosing not to confide in those closest to him created a huge rippling effect of hurting people, and in the end his fall led to his suicide. He had others who would have embraced and helped him, but he chose not to move his friendship into an area of accountability. For whatever reason, he felt it wasn't safe for him to do so, or perhaps he simply wanted to continue down an unhealthy path. Pray your messed up men become transparent with those closest to them.

3. *Confession, prayer, and "walking with" are vital.* "Confess your sins to one another, and pray for one another so that you may be healed" (James 5:16). Here's how it works: (1) The man recognizes he needs help in a certain area of his life. (2) He takes steps to get that help. (3) To keep himself on the right path, he may reach out to an accountability partner—another man who can walk with him. That person might be someone who has found success in working through the same issue. Think of an alcoholic who has a sponsor.

There are other ways a man can find accountability. Support groups, for instance, provide opportunity for weekly meetings with a group of the same gender. It's a safe setting in which men can gain insight and encouragement, celebrate each other's victories, pray with each other, stand by each other through challenges and temptations, and openly confess, "I blew it this week!" knowing that other men struggling with the same issue will understand.

In the end, interpersonal accountability for men, as for women, comes down to this: "Do two walk together unless they have agreed to do so?" (Amos 3:3 NIV).

What Part Do We Play?

Now that we understand a little more about accountability for men, some of you are thinking, "Does this mean we women can't ask the tough questions?" Absolutely not.

Several years after my father stopped drinking, his behavior led my mother to think he was drinking again. That moment was like hitting a large red button that set off sirens in my mom's mind. Though she addressed the issue with my dad, she wasn't sure he was being truthful.

Mom confessed her anxiety to me during a visit, so I took note of my dad's behavior. One afternoon, I pulled him into a room, held his hands, looked deep into his eyes, and asked, "Did you start drinking again?" Shock and confusion showed on his face; he confessed he felt a little out of sorts but had not turned back to alcohol.

A doctor's visit revealed that side effects from a new medicine were affecting his behavior. The doctor altered the meds and all was well. Sometimes we need to ask tough questions, and that's okay. However, I didn't try to keep my father accountable by spying on him, following him around, or anything like that. God's timing reveals truth. Had my dad been drinking, the problem would have surfaced. God brings things out of the darkness and into the light.

God desires that neither our men nor we ourselves suffer, struggle, or face our issues alone. He wants us to learn to lean on one another, pray for one another, and restore one another gently so that we may be healed. Give kudos to the men in your life who find much-needed accountability partners. Don't worry when they spend time together. If their time produces healing, fruit, and change, then praise God!

Jesus and the Messed Up Man

What happens if the messed up man in your life already blew it? One of the hardest things for women is watching men mess up, fall, fail, and embarrass themselves, others, and you. Ladies, come on! We have stories we can share. I've heard these words and said them myself: "Who is keeping you accountable?" It's easy for women to throw that in a man's face, especially when she feels he's messing up. Sound familiar?

Regretfully, I never step back to empathize with how Dave may feel about his mess-up or my condescending tone. I simply open mouth and turn on spout. I'm surprised at what comes out of it and how long I sometimes allow the spout to run.

When I look back at Judas and what he did to Jesus in the garden of Gethsemane, I find one surprising word. It is hidden among the tension, trauma, and emotions. *If I were in Jesus's sandals, I think, I couldn't say that word.* Animosity, hurt, and disgust would roar in my aching soul. Yet Jesus said it: he called Judas *friend.*

What kind of friend kisses you on the cheek while soldiers linger in the background with swords and clubs? Yet of all possible responses, Jesus said to him, "Friend, do what you have come for" (Matt. 26:50). He didn't look upon Judas in a different light, with less love, affection, or value than He had before. He loved Judas as much as He had always loved him. Seventeenth-century preacher Robert South put it like this:

> We have seen here the demeanor of friendship between man and man: but how is it, think we now, between Christ and the soul that depends upon Him? Is He anyways short in these offices of tenderness and mitigation? No, assuredly: but by infinite degrees superior. For where our heart does relent, His melts; where our eye pities, His bowels yearn. How many forwardnesses of ours does He smother, how many indignities does He pass by, with how many affronts does He put up at our hands, because His love is invincible, and His friendship unchangeable.[3]

Yes, Jesus's friendship is unchangeable, and we see that in His relationship with Judas. I dare not fret because God loves this man in my life so much more than I. God's passion is to transform him into a great disciple, teacher, minster of the gospel, and above all, friend.

What Can Women Do?

As women we can come alongside each other to help instill healthy behavior, suggest positive actions, and celebrate significant, praiseworthy moments. Rather than jumping into a man-bashing session, we can encourage each other to do the right things.

What then should our role be while God is working on the messed up men in our life? Ask God and your friends to keep you accountable in the following four areas. Doing these things may facilitate success for the messed up man and you.

1. Accept Him as He Is

"Therefore, accept one another, just as Christ also accepted us to the glory of God" (Rom. 15:7).

By deciding to accept the messed up man in your life just as he is, and by understanding that God is still perfecting a good work in him, we are released to love him the way God intended. Granted, there are days we don't like our messed up men, much less accept them. It may take running around the house in our pink fuzzy slippers shouting, "I accept him today, Lord. I accept him today," teeth grinding and arms flailing. This doesn't mean we accept his messes, behavior, or sins; we work through the impact of those things in our life. But we continue to accept the man himself as God does; we choose to see him as God sees him—a friend and a son.

2. Be Kind and Compassionate

"Be kind to one another, tender-hearted, forgiving each other, just as God in Christ also has forgiven you" (Eph. 4:32).

One coworker said, "Patience, Tina." *I'm just trying to help*, I thought. "It's a virtue, you know," he boasted. I wanted to respond like this: Humph! Arms folded, jaw clenched, storming off. Instead, I quietly slipped away and allowed him to work, thinking nothing more of our encounter until this moment. Truth is, he was right. Patience, kindness, and acceptance are often hard to find, and admitting when you're lacking in those areas can be even more difficult.

Accepting messed up men releases the emotions we need that help us extend kindness, compassion, and forgiveness. Kindness and compassion lead to forgiveness. Think about it. Our lack of kindness, or acceptance, is usually tied to some kind of negative emotion. Work through hidden anger, bitterness, and attitudes that keep you from embracing the man in your life. Perhaps his lack of accountability has hurt you, and you're unable to accept him until you've worked through your own hurt. Once you've tackled your own issues, acceptance and extending kindness will be much easier.

3. Love Unconditionally

"Let love be without hypocrisy" (Rom. 12:9).

Real love. What is it? It's not false, pretend, or restrained. Love goes for it—plunging in, perhaps face first instead of feet first. How do we get there? Through Christ. This love is different from accepting. We can accept someone into our space and yet never extend love. We love this way because Christ first loved us, and through Him we are able to love boundlessly and without limits. Allow God to convict and remind us to love, and stir our hearts when needed.

Have your accountability partner remind you when she sees you extending either love or hurt. Loving when we don't feel like it is hard; loving when we've been hurt is even harder. That's why we need God to hold us accountable and overflow His love into the fibers of our being. Only then will we be able to love without hypocrisy.

4. Encourage

"Therefore encourage one another and build up one another, just as you also are doing" (1 Thess. 5:11).

We've accepted, extended kindness, and even gotten to the point where we can express love. But can we encourage—boost, cheer, hearten? Encourage the man in your life to seek counsel, share struggles, and move toward building accountability. Build up the messed up man. Note praiseworthy moments and strive to become his loudest cheerleader.

Second Corinthians 9:8 says, "God is able to bless you abundantly, so that in all things at all times, having all that you need, you will abound in every good work" (NIV). I want to "abound in every good work," don't you? Especially in front of God. And look at that—God gives us everything we need in order to do so. He is "able to bless" us, and his "able" becomes our ABLE: through Christ we are able to Accept, Be kind, Love, and Encourage.

You Are ABLE

Accept him as he is.

Be kind and compassionate.

Love unconditionally.

Encourage.

"And God is **ABLE** to bless you abundantly, so that in all things at all times, having all that you need, you will abound in every good work." (2 Cor. 9:8 NIV)

Moving Beyond the Mess

1. How would you define *accountability?*

2. When it comes to women and messed up men, what role do you feel women have, if any, in helping to keep men accountable?

3. Why do you suppose Judas kept his struggle to himself? Describe his character. How were his actions consistent with his character? Disregarding the unique aspects of his betrayal, were his general actions consistent with how many men respond in today's world?

4. Do you feel men have a hard time finding other trustworthy men to help keep them accountable? If so, what are some possible reasons?

5. How can women help men succeed in developing accountability with other men? (For example, allow time with friends, encourage "man getaways," invite couples over that might spark a friendship with the other man.)

6. *Moving to a healthier place:* Time for accountability. Look back over the listings and Scriptures in the "What Can Women Do?"

section. Which area do you struggle with the most? Which Scripture reference can you hold on to that might help you the most in this area? What hope can women take away from these areas?

———————

May the Lord keep you accountable in the way you should live.

———————

May God give you the strength to release the men in your life to Him.

———————

And may you find peace in the process.

10

Samson

A Lustful Leader

*When lust has conceived, it gives birth to sin; and when
sin is accomplished, it brings forth death.*

JAMES 1:15

DAVE ❦ What single characteristic comes to mind when you think of Samson? Most of us who are familiar with Samson's story would define his life as one of great strength. After all, he killed a lion with just his bare hands, and a thousand men with the jawbone of a donkey. He carried the doors of a city gate to the top of a hill. For his final feat, he displaced the pillars holding up the roof of a great Philistine temple, killing all who were present, including himself. No doubt about it: Samson was a man of tremendous physical power. But he was also a man of great moral weakness—and that weakness was his downfall.

Samson's entire life is narrated in just four chapters in the book of Judges (13–16). An angel visited Manoah and his barren wife with the news that Samson (the name means "Man of the Sun") would be born to them. God's purpose for Samson's life was made clear to his parents: "The boy shall be a Nazirite to God from the womb; and he shall begin to deliver Israel from the hands of the Philistines" (Judg. 13:5). The Philistines had been oppressing Israel for forty years, and Samson was born to begin their liberation. The text makes clear that, as a Nazirite from birth, he was to be separated unto God and abide by a list of prohibitions that included not touching dead bodies; not drinking wine, grape juice, or even eating grapes; and never cutting his hair.

But the story has hardly begun when the eyes of Israel's deliverer fall upon a beautiful young Philistine woman. "Samson went down to Timnah and saw a woman in Timnah, one of the daughters of the Philistines. So he came back and told his father and mother, 'I saw a woman in Timnah, one of the daughters of the Philistines; now therefore, get her for me as a wife'" (Judg. 14:1–2).

Mom and dad protest, but Samson gets his way. In the very next verse, something jumps out at me. Samson says to his father, "Get her for me, for she looks good to me." The theme repeats itself in verse 7: "[Samson] went down and talked to the woman; and she looked good to Samson." Many of men's problems begin with that phrase, "She looks good." It is a stronger motivator for Samson than his purpose to "deliver Israel from the hands of the Philistines."

If your man struggles with sexual integrity, then this is where his issue will begin as well: "she looks good." And let me be clear, "she looks good" can often overrule all sense of judgment and rational thought.

Fred Stoeker, in his book *Every Heart Restored*, puts it this way:

> Men come hardwired with certain qualities that make it very tough to remain sexually pure. We don't need a date or a mistress—our male eyes give us the ability to sin just about anytime we want. All we need is a long, lingering look at a partially clothed or unclothed female body to receive a jolt of sexual pleasure. We aren't picky, either. The jolt can come just as easily from staring at the tight sweater on the girl on the bus . . . as it can from a romantic interlude with our wife. In short, we have a visual ignition switch when it comes to the female anatomy, and it takes very little to flip it on.[1]

Samson's ignition revved at high speed. Later on, Scripture says that Samson fell in love, but not with this Philistine woman of Timnah. This time it was all about the looks.

Jesus understood how difficult it would be for a man to keep his natural male inclinations in check. Sitting on the mountain among his band of rugged men, He told them, "You have heard that it was said, 'YOU SHALL NOT COMMIT ADULTERY'; but I say to you that everyone who looks at a woman with lust for her has already committed adultery with her in his heart" (Matt. 5:27–28). Men who struggle with sexual integrity can have a successful journey in this area if they choose.

The Eyes Have It

TINA ❧ I cleaned houses during college to help pay my way through school. Not until after a few months of cleaning did I realize that one of the couples I worked for had separated. I was now cleaning for the man of the house. One day I entered the living room, switched on the TV, and gasped in horror. I had stumbled upon his Playboy channel that he no doubt spent the previous evening watching. I never saw anything like it. Racing to turn it off, I tripped over everything in my path. A few weeks later, I stopped cleaning his home.

Ladies, are we naive about how many men struggle with sexual integrity? Walk down the halls of our churches and we'll pass men with tightly sealed secrets. Do you scratch your head and wonder why they don't use Nancy Reagan's phrase "Just say no"? Or Job's approach: "I made a covenant with my eyes not to look lustfully at a young woman" (Job 31:1 NIV)? How can turning an eye be so difficult?

Stoeker says, "Men receive a natural chemical high from looking at pictures of nude women. When our eyes lock onto images of nude women, pleasure chemicals bathe the limbic pleasure centers in the brain, and because it feels good, we want to come back for another hit (look). Quite often then, our addictive behaviors are not rooted in some lack of love for our wives. Rather, they're linked to the pleasure highs triggered by the images entering the eyes."[2]

Okay, let's get real. We know how it feels to walk down the candy aisle or pass the pastry section. I catch myself turning an eye toward that chocolate cake and then turning away saying, "No, no, no, Tina, that's not good for you." Sometimes I'm so proud of myself for walking away, but I confess there are moments of weakness when I look down at the cart only to find my lustful passion glaring back at me. In fact, at this very moment, my mouth is salivating over the thought of a sweet apple fritter. It wouldn't be so bad except I promised the doctor I would get off sweets. That's how it is with men. Hear me well: I'm not comparing women to an overstuffed doughnut or a skinny candy bar, and I'm not minimizing a man's issue with sexual integrity. I'm saying it's the passion, the lusting after something, that gets us. If the doctor says, "No more sweets, no alcohol, and no smoking," and your lustful cravings get the better of you, is that sin? When Dr. God says, "Don't do this," and we do it anyway, is that sin? The apostle John writes, "Everything in the world—the lust of the flesh, the lust of the eyes, and the pride of life—comes not from the Father but from the world" (1 John 2:16 NIV). When we live in the flesh, our worldly passions overpower our spiritual desires.

If I polled a hundred women and asked, "What do you lust after?" what would I hear? A roll in the hay with Brad Pitt or the hunk down the street. Sweets, cigarettes, alcohol, chocolate, and here's one—Starbucks! Oh yes! I crave a tall, salted caramel mocha (great with an apple fritter). Anyone who's had a salted caramel mocha understands it's the salt that makes the beverage so appealing. When the season ends, I dread having to wait another year.

What's *your* pleasure? Because surely you have at least one. We often look at a man's lust for women differently from the lust women have after things in their lives. But all of us lust, both men and women. Eve lusted after a piece of fruit she felt would make her wise; the Israelites lusted after their parents' false idols; and in Romans, Paul writes about men and women committing shameful lustful acts with one another. From a piece of fruit to sexual acts, we all lust after something.

Though women may never understand a man's response to the female body, we can easily understand the desire to have something we shouldn't and how it only takes one look for us to fall into that temptation.

The Women in Samson's Life

Few women stood out in Samson's life. He didn't have multiple wives or concubines. He didn't have sisters or aunts named in Scripture. What we do find are a handful of women who influenced Samson's life and whose lives he influenced. Let's take a look at them.

The Mother—Loyal, Nurturing, Prayerful

God gave Samson to his parents as a gift, a miracle. How did his previously barren mother feel about this child, especially knowing how she received him? If we were given that gift, we would want to honor the Giver. Samson's mother did as the Lord instructed.

Mothers understand how difficult it is to keep kids within certain boundaries. While we melt over snippets of hair in blue and pink plastic frames, Samson was never allowed to cut his hair. And no eating anything off the vine—no halving grapes for a little toddler to scoop up and mash in his mouth. The last requirement probably didn't pose as much of a problem: he couldn't touch dead bodies.

Now imagine Samson empowered by the Holy Spirit every day of his life. I envision him looking like Arnold Schwarzenegger from *Conan the Barbarian* and wearing dreadlocks like the Jamaican singer Bob Marley. What a sight! I'm sure he towered over his mom. Proud parents beamed on their son as he grew taller, broader, and stronger. But one day everything changed.

It's every parent's nightmare, sensing that their child is turning from God. Samson's character reflected so much of what young adults go through in today's world as they step outside their upbringing, test the waters, and rebel in their own way in order to find their place. Through it all, God still used Samson. But Samson's actions impacted his mother, as any son's would affect any mother. And it all started with his lust for a woman.

The Bride—Young, Innocent, Beautiful

Samson made a trip to Timnah and laid eyes on a stunning but thoroughly pagan Philistine. His decision to marry her was driven by pure lust. Mothers who've been there are shaking their heads, "No, no, no!" Samson's mom tried talking sense into him, but Samson stood his ground and married the girl anyway.

Though we don't really know the bride's age, we can assume she was young. She had no idea whom she was marrying. She had no idea that Samson would keep secrets, throw tantrums, put her in a compromising position, and murder her people. And why would he care? In biblical times, women went from being their father's property to being their husband's property. But though this young girl understood her position, it didn't take away the pain of the wound.

This young girl's life was about to change. Her heart had no idea of its upcoming wounding, not only by her husband but also by her desperate people. Sometimes I scratch my head and ask, "Really, God? This is Your plan? You threw this poor, innocent girl into the mix of Samson's mess?" But then I'm reminded that God works in all things.

From the beginning of the wedding, Samson revealed his messed up character. We can discern the hallmarks of a flesh-driven man, and in particular, of a man who struggled with sexual integrity.

Out of Bounds. The law required that Jews marry Jews; a Jewish man married within his own religion. But Samson didn't care that he was a Jewish Nazirite and his wife an unbelieving Philistine. When a man struggles with sexual integrity, he steps outside his boundaries.

Please don't misunderstand me; if you married an unbeliever or someone from a different culture, that doesn't mean he struggles with sexual integrity. But men who struggle with sexual integrity also easily ignore healthy boundaries. A lustful glance at a young Philistine girl caused Samson to violate his restrictions.

Lack of Intimacy. Samson didn't set the tone for intimacy early on in his marriage. He told a riddle to a group of men from the wedding party and chose not to disclose the answer to his bride. Samson married her to meet a need other than intimacy. Men who struggle with sexual integrity have a difficult time creating intimacy. They are disconnected from themselves as well as from the woman in their lives. Samson's first all-about-Samson moment in his marriage meant disregarding his new bride, which of course he would have done if he thought of her as mere property meant to fulfill his lust.

Tantrums. We all throw tantrums in one form or another. Just because your messed up man throws a tantrum doesn't mean he's struggling with sexual integrity. However, men who struggle with this issue also have a difficult time keeping their other emotions under control. When Samson heard the Philistine men tell the secret to the riddle, he blew a fuse. He paid the debt, honoring the terms of the riddle, but he took it out on the Philistines by killing thirty of their men. Afterward, Samson isolated himself by returning to his parents' house and leaving his new bride behind. Later he came back for her and a tumble in the bedroom only to learn she had been given to his best man at the wedding. After another chaotic moment in Samson's out-of-control life, his now ex-bride paid the price for his behavior. The Philistine men did as they said and burned her and her father to death.

The Lover—Enticing, Luxurious, Deceiving

After meeting a physical need with a prostitute, Samson came upon another woman and fell in love. Yes, "it came about that he loved a woman in the valley of Sorek, whose name was Delilah" (Judg. 16:4).

Delilah must have been a beauty. People are consistent; without the proper healing in their lives, they do what they've always done, act how they've always acted, and speak and think according to their messed up lives. Samson certainly did. His first wife had to pass the beauty test, and no doubt Delilah did as well.

Delilah made Samson weak in the knees but not in his willingness to spill the beans about his strength. How did it happen? Imagine Samson cozy in the arms of his lover while she stroked his long locks. She asked, "Tell me the secret of your great strength and how you can be tied up and subdued" (Judg. 16:6 NIV). Come on, girls, where do a man's thoughts go from that question! I can hear Samson now: "Where's the rope?"

Samson responded with a series of inventive lies (another characteristic of someone struggling with sexual integrity), and eventually Delilah questioned his love for her. Then, just like that, love spilled all. Of
course Delilah did not reciprocate Samson's love; she was scheming to
help his enemies capture him. This sad, sorrowful mess of a woman
was willing to betray her lover for money. And Samson had no idea his
sexual compromise would lead him to place his God-given power in the
hands of a woman.

The impact of Samson's choices and actions cost him his life. And
so it is with countless men today. Their lack of sexual integrity packs
a big punch and its ripple effect can cost them their jobs, families, and
futures.

Though I'm not saying Samson struggled with a sexual addiction, I
do want to share a list of characteristics Mark Laaser shares in his book,
The Secret Sin: Healing the Wounds of Sexual Addiction:

1. Preoccupation with sexual behaviors
2. Escalating patterns of sexual activity
3. Acting distant or withdrawn
4. Depression and mood swings
5. Irritability
6. Abuse of self or others
7. Resistance to supervision or criticism
8. Use of sexual humor
9. Inappropriate sexual behavior and overt sexual advances
10. Occupational, social, family, professional, and legal difficulties
11. Intuition
12. Direct evidence[3]

Samson's abuse of others, along with his irritability, mood swings,
rage, tantrums, emotional distance from his bride, and escalating patterns of sexual activity—from his wife, to a prostitute, to his lover—
point to some of the above characteristics. Samson also had difficulties
with his family, social life, and life in general.

Spiraling Downward

DAVE ✖ As you can see, Samson's life spiraled out of control, and he responded to his circumstances chaotically and violently. Samson threw tantrums, killed innocent people, and deserted his "looks good" bride. Yet in the midst of it all, God was at work. At least four times we read in the Scriptures that the "Spirit of the Lord" was moving through Samson (Judg. 13:24–25; 14:6, 19; 15:14). This may be a head-scratcher. God is empowering Samson, blessing him even in the midst of some extremely ungodly behavior.

Jesus said that God "causes His sun to rise on the evil and the good, and sends rain on the righteous and the unrighteous" (Matt. 5:45). This means that God operates on a whole different level than we do. He will accomplish His purpose through anyone and everyone He chooses, even if they are not worthy of the honor. God will use the messed up man in your life to accomplish His purposes. But while it may appear that God is blessing the unrighteous, we will see in Samson's story that the wages of sin is still death.

The Impact

TINA ✖ Standing on the sidelines, experiencing the impact of a man's issue with sexual integrity, is like having rotten eggs thrown at you. You never know when they're coming or where they will land. The first blow hits hard and you're flung off balance. The pain is unbearable. You stumble to your feet. Standing is difficult. The stench and dirtiness overwhelm you, yet you persevere and maintain your position.

Over time you learn to dodge a few throws, adjust by swaying here and there, or you put up a few shields to block the blows. And when you do get hit, it doesn't seem as painful because you've been through it so often that you become immune to the pain. Now you expect the blows, wait for them to come, and justify the man's actions. Yet you still believe him when he says, "This will be the last time"—even though, deep down, you know it will not—because you *want* to hope.

For other women, the more strikes you endure, the angrier you become. Before long, the least little thing causes you to explode and unleash wrath. Bitterness eats at your insides like a fast-moving flame. You hate. You hate life. You hate him. You hate yourself. His actions have changed you. Sickened you. Turned you into something you never thought you'd become.

The ripple effect of a man's sexual sin is devastating. Unfortunately, in today's world, opportunities to compromise one's sexual integrity are as easily obtainable as the products in a grocery store aisle. Nearly universal access to the Internet makes resisting temptation much more difficult.

The following information was reported by the American Academy of Matrimonial Lawyers in 2002. The survey reveals the impact of the Internet on divorce:[4]

+ 68 percent of divorces involved one party meeting a new lover on the Internet.
+ 56 percent involved one party having "an obsessive interest in pornographic websites.
+ 47 percent involved excessive time on the computer.
+ 33 percent involved excessive time in chat rooms.

Besides the anger women feel when betrayed, here are a few more gut-busting thoughts and emotions they may experience:

I'm not beautiful enough.
I didn't give him enough attention.
I wasn't "love worthy."
I deserved it.
I'll never get over it.
It's my fault.
I feel sickened that he would touch another woman (affair), look at another woman (pornography), or talk to another woman (phone sex), and then me.
I fear the future.

The Healing

We cannot fix the messed up man in our life; only God can do that. But we can take steps to heal. I had a friend whose husband inherited boxes of old *Playboy* magazines. Those classics sat in his garage for years. When I asked my friend how she felt about them and whether she could talk to her husband about them, she replied, "He doesn't see anything wrong with them." Because of his attitude, she believed her hands were tied to do anything about them.

What a dilemma! What do we do about our messed up man acting out, especially when he sees nothing wrong with it? Unless the Holy Spirit convicts your messed up man's heart and opens his eyes, nothing will change. We can talk till our last word is uttered, but unless he's ready to make a change, there's nothing the woman can do to change him.

However, all hope is not lost. Here are a few things you can do to get yourself in a healthy place.

Open your heart. Our emotions need a home, a place to go, somewhere to turn. So often we make bad choices about how to deal with our crushing feelings. We lash back, allow bitterness to fester, or deny how we feel altogether. Determine to find a safe place to release your emotions, and to work on you and the issues at hand.

Give yourself permission to heal and forgive. You don't have to pretend it didn't happen or think you need to get up the next day and act like you've forgiven him because that's what good Christian girls do. In due time, as your heart heals and with God's help, you can come to a place of forgiveness. Every step, tiny or not, leads somewhere. Give yourself time and permission to heal; forgiveness will follow.

Find a trusted support system. Often our mind-set is, "I don't need help. It's not my issue." Part of finding strength and coping with a man's sexual betrayal is finding a good support system. Choose wisely, my friends, because whom you confide in can be beneficial or detrimental. There are many wonderful Christian counselors and support groups for women experiencing this issue. Find someone who will instill biblical truths and offer hope.

Come to understand the battle. Men struggling with sexual integrity wrestle against the flesh. Matthew says, "The spirit is willing, but the flesh is weak" (26:41). But there is often a deeper reason men act out sexually apart from any pleasure they may receive from the act. Men struggling with sexual addiction often have issues with abandonment, sexual abuse, lack of nurturing, and so on. As with any struggle, men make unhealthy choices to fill voids in their life. Once in recovery, they address these issues, get to the heart of the matter, and learn to replace unhealthy choices with healthy ones. Women walking with men in this area need to understand the battle, and through that understanding, women will come away with a greater understanding of what they need to work on.

Move forward. Often we feel the need to put our lives on hold until the messed up man's life gets straightened out. Don't. Spend time praying about your situation and God will direct.

Finally, remember the words of Isaiah:

> "Fear not; you will no longer live in shame. Don't be afraid; there is no more disgrace for you. . . . For your Creator will be your husband; the Lord of Heaven's Armies is his name! He is your Redeemer . . . the God of all the earth. For the Lord has called you back from your grief—as though you were a young wife abandoned by her husband," says your God.
>
> "For the mountains may move and the hills disappear, but even then my faithful love for you will remain." (Isa. 54:4–6, 10 NLT)

The Pillars

DAVE ❦ How did it happen—that moment of weakness that cost Samson his life? Was it the embrace of a lover? A room scented with perfume and clouded with passion?

The gentle stroke of a feminine finger on the temple, the sweet fragrance of a woman, the lavish softness of her lap—such things can turn a man's head to mush.

> [Delilah] made him sleep on her knees, and called for a man and had him shave off the seven locks of his hair. Then she began to afflict him, and his strength left him. She said, "The Philistines are upon you, Samson!" And he awoke from his sleep and said, "I will go out as at other times and shake myself free." But he did not know that the Lord had departed from him. (Judg. 16:19–20)

Isn't it a sad picture? The strong man became weak. The Lord departed, and Samson didn't even know it. I suppose he still looked strong, and his muscle mass was still in place. Yet in a moment he had become powerless at the hands of a woman.

"Then the Philistines seized him and gouged out his eyes" (v. 21). I find it ironic that the man who was led into ruin by his eyes ("she looks good") in the end lost his ability to see. Samson was led into destructive relationships with his eyes, and the price was high—blindness. Your messed up man will also likely face a high price for his wandering eyes. His strength may be removed and his power may grow weak.

"However, the hair of his head began to grow again after it was shaved off" (v. 22). I love that Samson's story doesn't end with a bald head and blind eyes. God wasn't through with Samson, and He isn't through with your messed up man. God is a God of grace and second chances.

Samson spent his time in prison and as a laughingstock before the Philistines. But one day a young boy took his hands and brought Samson before the Philistines to "amuse them." Samson said to the boy, "Let me feel the pillars on which the house rests, that I may lean against them" (v. 26). Pillars represent strength, and they literally hold the house up; Samson's final victory involved displacing the pillars and bringing the house down. Your man will likely have to push some pillars out of his life in order to defeat his demons and bring his enemies down. It may appear to be the end of him, but God knows how to resurrect and restore.

Samson's story ends not with a shame-filled, broken-down old man rotting in a Philistine prison; it ends heroically, with a strong Samson bringing down the Temple of Dagon with his bare hands, and in the process killing more of the enemy in his death than he did in his life.

How does God view Samson, who lived so foolishly and so full of lust? In Hebrews 11, we have the "Hall of Faith," a listing of great men and women of God: Abel, Noah, Abraham, Joseph, Rahab, David . . . sixteen in all. Included in their number is the "Man of the Sun," Samson. Hebrews 11:39 says that he and all of the rest gained approval through their faith.

So again the question: What single characteristic comes to mind when you think of Samson? Strength? Weakness? Lust?

If you ask God, His answer will be—Samson is a man of faith.

The Pillars

"Let me feel the pillars on which the house rests, that I may lean against them." (Judges 16:26)

Pillars represent strength, and they literally hold the house up.

Pray God tears down the strongholds and erects strong pillars of faith.

Moving Beyond the Mess

1. How would you define lust?
2. Read James 1:14–15. What things do you lust after or "have a strong desire for"? Be honest.
3. What did James mean when he said, "Then when lust has

conceived, it gives birth to sin; and when sin is accomplished, it brings forth death" (1:15)? How does this relate to Samson's story?

4. Read 1 Corinthians 10:12. What does the Scripture say to do? How can following the Scripture's advice help women come alongside men struggling with sin? Though men are responsible for their own behavior, do you think women dressing more modestly could make a difference? What other actions can women take to encourage sexual integrity?

5. Read Romans 13:14. What does the Bible say lust belongs to? How are we to fight lust? How can we do that?

6. *Moving to a healthier place:* Read Galatians 6:1. How difficult would it be for a woman wounded by a man's lack of sexual integrity to do this? Read these Scriptures that help women move beyond the wound and into a healthier place: Job 32:8; Psalms 37:34; 119:50; 147:3; Proverbs 24:29.

May the Lord help you find healing and restoration. May He cleanse and renew your relationships, and may you come to find a greater strength within you.

The Demoniac

An Oppressed Outcast

*It was for freedom that Christ set us free; therefore keep
standing firm and do not be subject again to a yoke of slavery.*
GALATIANS 5:1

"Hush, be still!" The wind died down and the crashing of the waves
ceased. Silence—except the sound of water sloshing over the disciples'
feet. They sat, dumbfounded. In almost a whisper, one said, "Who is
this, that even the wind and the sea obey Him?"

Sunlight glistened off the glassy waters. The boat completed its
crossing in peace and slid onto the far shore.

But at the place where they had landed, at the edge of a cemetery, a
different kind of storm was raging. For he lived there—this man, this
tormented soul, there among the dead. Naked, he wandered among the
tombs, shrieking at the sky, the scars of his self-abuse crisscrossing his
filthy skin. Locals, even family members, steered far from him, fearing
his madness, his terrifying, unreasoning violence.

But Jesus did not fear. Into the heart of the graveyard He stepped as one with full authority and the right to be there, and before Him the darkness scattered.

"Come out of him, unclean spirit."

Rushing from behind the tomb where he had been hiding, the man threw himself at the feet of Jesus. "What business do we have with each other, Jesus, Son of the Most High God? I beg You, do not torment us!" The man's voice—*their* voice—resounded through the hills. The demons knew Him and trembled in His presence.

"What is your name?" Jesus demanded.

"My name is Legion, for we are many."

A Legion of Names

TINA In J. R. R. Tolkien's classic *The Hobbit*, Gandalf tells the dwarves of a strange being named Beorn who will give them food, water, and a place to rest. But who is this Beorn? Gandalf replies, "He is a skin-changer. He changes his skin; sometimes, he is a huge black bear, sometimes he is a great strong black-haired man." Gandalf adds, "He is under no enchantment but his own."[1]

The story of the demoniac is the story of a man taken hostage—bound—through demon possession. Today men continue to experience various forms of bondage and, like Beorn, spells of their own creation. Strongholds create skin-changers: one minute they're strong men; the next, something else. My father was like that. Sober, he could be reasoned with, but under the influence of alcohol he became a bear, savage and unpredictable.

Strongholds are destructive, ongoing behaviors that eventually lead to destruction. Alcohol and drug addiction are just two examples. Others, such as sex, greed, anger, control, fear, and jealousy, all have a similar potential to take a man captive.

But something happens when we confess a stronghold in our life. Perhaps that's why Jesus asks the demon to say his name, even though Jesus already knew it—because names play important roles in our lives. That's why in recovery programs, it's common to hear, "Hello. My name is John and I'm an alcoholic." Speaking the truth about the bondage brings the stronghold out of the darkness and into the light and weakens its grasp on a person.

What strongholds clutch the men in your life? Though a demon may not hold your man hostage, other things in his life can—things we've already mentioned, and any other sin that pulls him its way and entraps him.

Legion

DAVE ❧ Tina has brought to life the story in Luke 8:26–39 of one really messed up man. Possessed by a multitude of demons, he wore no clothes, had no house, and lived among the tombs in a cemetery in the country of the Gerasenes. He had been chained up many times and even guarded, but the demons in him were so strong that the man would break the chains and wander out into the desert. He was called Legion because of the many demons that possessed him. This tormented man lived utterly alone—no friends, no family, no shelter, no life.

I don't know the condition of the man in your life. I don't know his stronghold, whether he's possessed by an evil spirit or just struggling to do the right thing. He may be at the end of some great calamity or at the very beginning. Or maybe he appears to be doing just fine. I think everybody struggles with something, maybe many things, and some more than others. Like the demoniac, your man may be dealing with a legion of issues.

I concluded early in the process of writing this book that not only am I a messed up man, but to some degree I could be a prime example for each of the issues in these chapters. Though I have never been possessed by a multitude of demons, I have been possessed by a myriad of issues. I am Legion—I have many problems! Through years of work, I've overcome in many areas, but believe me, I'm still working at it. Let me share a couple things about the Gerasene demoniac that give me hope and may do so for you as well.

First, before Jesus arrived in the land of the Gerasenes, he was already headed in that direction. Previously He had been teaching a large crowd by the Sea of Galilee—a beautiful place with much history, where the disciples fished for food and Jesus for men. "When evening came, He said to [his disciples], 'Let us go over to the other side.' Leaving the crowd, they took Him along with them in the boat, just as He was; and other boats were with Him" (Mark 4:35–36).

Consider for a moment: When Jesus said, "Let us go over to the other side," was He trying to get away from the crowd or step into a moment for restoration—or was He up to something more?

Jesus knew what the other side held. Jesus was on a mission. Here's one *big* point of this story in a few words: *Jesus pursues us.*

You may not see Jesus in your situation yet, but He is on His way. I love the fact that between casting off from Galilee and docking in the land of the Gerasenes, Jesus calmed a storm. Perhaps He was warming up for the storm of demons He would soon confront. We have to trust that Jesus had His priorities in the correct order, even if we would have done things differently. As Proverbs 3:5 says, "Trust in the Lord with all your heart and do not lean on your own understanding."

Second, Jesus deals with essential issues first. He didn't clothe the naked man. He didn't provide shelter for him. He didn't even release him from his chains. The first thing Jesus did was free the man from demonic oppression, from his bondage, his stronghold. The lack of clothing and shelter was symptomatic of the man's real issue. Jesus dealt with that issue, knowing that everything else would be corrected as a result.

You may not see your own man's symptoms change right away. But rest assured, Jesus is working on what's most important.

Third, change is costly. "There was a herd of many swine feeding there on the mountain; and the demons implored Him to permit them to enter the swine. And He gave them permission. And the demons came out of the man and entered the swine; and the herd rushed down the steep bank into the lake and was drowned" (Luke 8:32–33).

The owners of the pigs paid a high price for the healing of a man they may not have valued or even known. You may likewise pay a price to see your man recover. You may have to change in the process of seeing your messed up man restored. His recovery may reveal hidden issues of your own which must be addressed. Through his healing process, you may discover that you yourself are a person with many problems.

The Family

TINA ✂ Somewhere in this world, the demoniac had a family. The Bible doesn't say whether he married or had children, but we do know he came from a village where "his people" dwelt. Imagine how embarrassed they must have felt once news hit that their relative was seen wandering naked among the tombs—a crazy man who had lost his senses, cutting himself with broken glass.

I imagine that early in his demonic state of mind, someone trudged over to the tombs to talk sense to him: "Come home. Please. We can help you." I'm only speculating, of course, and after a season of fruitless effort, I suppose everyone left him alone. But my point is, when a messed up man struggles with a stronghold, his family is greatly impacted. In the stories we read in the Bible, people who had no idea what to do with their afflicted family members brought them to Jesus. "When evening came, they brought to Him many who were demon-possessed; and He cast out the spirits with a word, and healed all who were ill" (Matt. 8:16).

To us, this task of shedding a stronghold might seem easy: "Why don't you just quit? Stop doing that." It's not that simple, though; for the struggling person, the battle is fierce. The stronghold can overpower a man's ability to break its grip. But praise God, when it comes face to face with Jesus, it falls to its knees, reveals its secret identity, and light forces out the darkness. There is release. Healing. Freedom.

The Deliverer

Beth Moore says, "God is far more interested in our getting to know the Deliverer than simply being delivered."[2] One year proved to be a valuable lesson for me in that area.

The years of my father's alcoholism were difficult and trying. As children we learned to keep silent about the issues in our family. The one time my sister and I tried sharing with the school counselor, the social worker called my parents before visiting our home. Upon her arrival, she found our family neatly ordered and everyone doing well. My sister and I looked like ignorant children trying to cause trouble rather than seeking help.

From that moment on we felt helpless, and hopeless that anyone would rescue us from our dire circumstances. Our next thought was to plan our escape—run away from home. That didn't pan out either.

One summer, right before my sixteenth birthday, I attended a summer youth camp. Little did I know God went before me, sending a speaker just for me. Sitting around the campfire with other kids singing songs like "Kumbaya," "Give Me Oil in My Lamp," and "I've Got Joy Down in My Heart," I was running on empty. Then it happened— the speaker's testimony. I hung on his every word, swallowing hard and choking down tears. *He was an alcoholic, too?* He shared his miraculous recovery, when God delivered him instantly. *How can it be?* Questions formed in my tangled mind, crowding, pushing. *I need to leave. I need to cry.*

I jumped up and ran away from the smoked-filled circle, tears streaming from my eyes. My departure did not go unnoticed. Afterward the speaker found me, touched my arm, and asked, "Would you like to talk?"

Sitting across from this young evangelist, I said it out loud: "My father's an alcoholic." Later I would make that admission to a group of people for the first time, but this moment was my moment of confession, reality, and coming to painful terms with my father's stronghold and its impact on me.

I must have cried a senseless amount of tears. The man encouraged me to never give up on my father. He reassured me that while the stronghold in my dad's life had changed him, God was a mighty God who, if my father was willing, would take back my dad's life and crush the stronghold.

That year at camp I found hope. I *witnessed* hope. And I came to believe in hope—that God would one day break the chains that bound my dad. It started when I saw, named, and thus exposed the stronghold. The ground shakes and heaven moves when that happens.

God's Way

Fast-forward to several years later—after I finished college, married, and settled down not far from my parents. Kids ran around the house and noise bounced off walls—the usual chaos of one of our family's Thanksgiving gatherings.

The phone rang and I answered. A familiar voice on the other end said, "This is your uncle." After chatting for a moment, he said, "Don't tell anyone yet, but I led your dad to the Lord."

What? Shocked, I whirled around and glared at my father. There he stood, or tried to stand, slurring his words while holding onto his drink. "You what?" I said to my uncle. *Am I the first to know? Does my mother know?* So many questions ran through my mind.

My heart sank. *Where is the miraculous healing? The change?* Joy did not bust through that day. Instead, despair grabbed hold. I felt my father didn't mean it. His old life stood before me. His stronghold taunted.

A few months later, my mother called to let me know my father stopped drinking the heavy stuff. He was now down to a few six packs a day. I snickered. "Well, okay, Mom."

Faith, where are you? When did I give up the hope I found at camp?

In the ensuing months, my mother called routinely to report on my father's alcohol consumption. Every month he drank less and less. Almost a year passed when the landmark call came: "Tina, your dad has been drinking only two beers a day, and today he went to the refrigerator, opened it up to get the last beer, and said, 'Beer makes me sick to my stomach. I don't think I'll drink anymore.'"

Later on my uncle shared the story of what happened between him and my father. My dad called him, and they met in the parking lot of an old, abandoned grocery store. My father said, "I can't do this anymore," and broke down. My uncle took his old Bible off the dashboard of his pickup truck and shared the gospel with my dad—how Jesus loved him, died for him, gave him purpose, and wanted to deliver him. My father prayed right there—on his knees in the dirty parking lot, cars driving by. He didn't care.

After that year, the Lord grabbed hold of my faithless heart. I believed God always did things in a certain way. Not true. I believed that in order for my dad to get better, he would need to check into a rehab facility. Not true. I also believed that if God didn't use rehab, then He would instantly remove my dad's bondage, just like He did for the demoniac or the camp evangelist. Not true.

The Lord had a heart-to-heart talk with me: "You see, Tina, my ways are not your ways, and my thoughts are not your thoughts. I can do things in ways you never dreamed possible."

Not until God revealed it to me did I realize that during that long year, God had been detoxing my father. Every day, my father drank a little less until he got down to just one beer. That was God's way.

God also worked on my father's habit of going to the bar. Slowly, my dad stepped away from his unhealthy daily routine. That was God's way.

My father worked on distancing himself from his drinking and fishing buddies, who were more about drinking than fishing. It took time—and it was also God's way.

I watched my father make those changes in his life. And I realized that God didn't save my father from his destructive life—God *was* saving him. Every day that my father made a change was a lifesaving moment.

On the phone with me one day, reliving that year when my father stopped drinking, my mother shared an important insight. After saying that alcohol made him sick, Dad took a huge step that symbolized something far greater than what he had done the entire year. Of his own will, he took that one last beer to the sink, opened it up, and poured it out. What a beautiful picture of releasing what once tried to destroy his life. He found complete freedom that day and a strength none of us knew he had. Of course, that moment didn't mean my dad never struggled, never craved another drink. It didn't mean the demon wouldn't call my father's name or find moments to push a bottle his way.

It meant that God was greater in my father than Satan, who is in the world (1 John 4:4).

My father was probably provoked by his demons more than I imagine, but he persevered. He went to church, read his Bible, and prayed. The days we had him as a changed man were days we will cherish the rest of our lives. My dad became a wonderful man, full of love, always giving back to others, and then one day God took him home. He is now experiencing freedom in a whole new way.

Perhaps you have misconceptions and doubts about the way God is caring for the messed up men in your life. Perhaps you've imagined God delivering him and working in his life in a certain way. I encourage you to not look away from small steps, as I did. Instead, take notice of those moments, trusting that God is doing something good.

Four Things to Pray That Help Tear Down Strongholds

I admire my mother, who never gave up on my father, prayed every day, and endured more than I can imagine. Somewhere in her mind she kept saying, "I know you can do this, Lord—I know you can do this." Perhaps over time her prayers changed from "I know you can do this, God" to "I know *he* can do this. He *can* do this. Give him strength."

Prayer is one of the major tools for changing a man's life. Matthew 3 tells us how we should pray and what we should pray for. Pray that God's will be done for you and the messed up man in your life. Ask God to strengthen you both with His daily bread, to forgive you and give you the ability to forgive others, to protect you from temptation, and above all, to deliver you and the messed up man from the Evil One.

Will you commit to pray through the following four areas every day for the messed up man in your life? Pray along these lines for your man.

That he be filled with the Spirit of God. Ask God to give him wisdom, understanding, and to increase his gifting and abilities. Ask God to reveal Himself in your man's everyday walk.

Scripture: "[God] has filled him with the Spirit of God, in wisdom, in understanding and in knowledge and in all craftsmanship" (Exod. 35:31).

Prayer: Dear Lord, fill _____ with Your Holy Spirit. Your Spirit forces out the enemy, releases its grasp, and brings _____ to his knees. May You sweep through every fiber and cell. Envelop him with Your wisdom and understanding. Take hold of his mind, body, and soul. Remove anything that's not from You, from his head to his toes. May You, and nothing else, be the one who resides in him. Save him, Lord. I hand him over to You, Lord, to do a great and mighty work. Amen.

That his sin would come into the light. Ask God to expose your man's stronghold. Though it may be a painful process, ask God to force the stronghold out of its hiding place and into God's glorious light, knowing that once in the light, the sin loses its power.

Scripture: "God is Light, and in Him there is no darkness at all. If we say that we have fellowship with Him and yet walk in the darkness, we lie and do not practice the truth; but if we walk in the Light as He Himself is in the Light, we have fellowship with one another, and the blood of Jesus His Son cleanses us from all sin" (1 John 1:5–7).

Prayer: Dear Lord, I ask that _____ find the courage to come out of the darkness and into the light. Open opportunities to reveal his stronghold. Bring others into his life with whom he feels confident and comfortable sharing. Release him of this burden to keep the stronghold a secret. Take away his shame and guilt. Replace it with a sense of Your love and forgiveness. Help him to become disgusted with the stronghold, and instill in him an urgency to repent, to get rid of it. Give him an aching desire to change. And through Your name, we claim victory in his life.

The battle has already been won. Give him the strength to claim victory. Amen.

That God becomes his stronghold. Pray that God would become the stronghold of your messed up man and that all else would be sent away.

> Scripture: "Because of his strength I will watch for You, for God is my stronghold" (Ps. 59:9).

> Prayer: Dear Lord, God of strength and courage, come quickly. We need You. I ask that You break the strongholds in _____ life; that You remove their grip, and that You become the one he grabs hold of. Replace his struggle with the power of Your will. I know that through You, he can do great things. Open his eyes to watch, seek, and find You. Strengthen his grasp on You. May it be so, Lord. May it be so. I praise You for what You're about to do in his life. Amen.

That God equips him for the battle. Pray for the man in your life to put on the full armor of God, and that through Christ he will continue to fight a victorious battle.

> Scripture: "Finally, be strong in the Lord and in the strength of His might. Put on the full armor of God, so that you will be able to stand firm against the schemes of the devil. For our struggle is not against flesh and blood, but against the rulers, against the powers, against the world forces of this darkness, against the spiritual forces of wickedness in the heavenly places" (Eph. 6:10–12).

> Prayer: Dear Lord, I ask for protection for me, my family, and _____. Surround us with Your mighty warriors and guard us day and night. May we put on our full armor, leaving nothing out, and may we stand firm against our enemy's

schemes. Bring those schemes to light, Lord, and remind us, during our flesh-filled moments, that we do not fight against each other but against spiritual forces. I ask that You not only change the man in my life, but me too. Rescue me, teach me, and bring me back to You. Together, may we do great things for Your kingdom. Amen.

Four Things to Pray That Help Tear Down Strongholds

Pray for God to

1. fill the messed up man with His Spirit;
2. bring the stronghold out of the darkness and into the light;
3. become the messed up man's stronghold; and
4. equip and protect the messed up man.

DAVE ❧ Two thousand swine died the day Jesus delivered the demoniac, just to give one man back his life. As you can imagine, chaos broke out, and people rushed to the scene to glimpse the commotion. What did they find? "They came to Jesus and observed the man who had been demon-possessed sitting down, clothed and in his right mind, the very man who had had the 'legion'" (Mark 5:15).

Imagine the people's shock and confusion. The man had become something more than what others knew him as—possessed. Did they know how to respond to a man whose stronghold had been stripped away and who now stood in the full glory of how God created him?

> As He [Jesus] was getting into the boat, the man who had been demon-possessed was imploring Him that he might accompany Him. And He did not let him, but He said to him, "Go

home to your people and report to them what great things
the Lord has done for you, and how He had mercy on you."
And he went away and began to proclaim in Decapolis what
great things Jesus had done for him; and everyone was amazed.
(Mark 5:18–20)

Here's the payoff: your man comes home! Rejoice! Praise! Worship!
However, the happily ever after might include a few caveats. Perhaps
you'll receive a bill in the mail for a thousand drowned pigs—maybe
even a lawsuit. Friends who walked with you through your crisis may
find themselves looking for the next person to help and begin to distance
themselves from you and your family. A house without a man must now
adjust to the homecoming of a husband and father and his desire to
play a significant role in the family with whom he has not previously
engaged. It's true that a lot will improve as your man returns home, but
don't think it will be easy. You will need to make adjustments.

However, hold on to hope that God *is* saving the messed up man in
your life. Not that he *will*, but He *is*. Every day of our life God saves
us from something. Paul reminds us that through Christ we have the
weapons we need to battle strongholds. Paul says, "The weapons we
fight with are not the weapons of the world. On the contrary, they have
divine power to demolish strongholds" (2 Cor. 10:4 NIV).

Remind yourself that God is coming and, indeed, is already present. He will battle the storms to get to your messed up man; He will
step through fields of death without trepidation; and He will look the
stronghold square in the eye and say, "Come out. Come out of him!" We
look forward to the day messed up men stand up and declare the great
things God has done.

Moving Beyond the Mess

1. What part of the demoniac's story stood out to you?
2. What are some of the strongholds men face in today's world? Do
   you know of someone with a stronghold? If you're discussing this
   in a group, share without using names (if you feel safe doing so).

3. Tina mentioned the difference between someone "battling" a stronghold and someone who has "given in" to their stronghold. What is your perception of that?

4. Do you believe God works in a certain way? Explain. What has been your experience of God's working in your life? Has it been consistent, or can you relate to God's working in ways we never expected? Give examples.

5. Families often want to rescue the one battling a stronghold. What can families do, or not do, to help?

6. Moving into a Healthier Place: Read through and talk about the "Four Things to Pray That Help Tear Down Strongholds." What can you add to the list? How can these prayers help women who live with men struggling with strongholds? There is a common thread throughout the prayers: for "God to . . ." How do these prayers help women realize they cannot fix the messed up men in their lives—only God can?

May the Lord give you strength to cope with and endure anything that may come your way. May God tear down strongholds and release the Enemy's grip—and may you see God's mighty deliverance.

12

Gideon

A Weak-Kneed Warrior

There is no fear in love; but perfect love casts out fear.
1 JOHN 4:18

DAVE ❦ I was around six or seven years old when I first felt the grip of real terror. My older brother took me to see the huge pile of boxes high school students had collected for the big homecoming bonfire—a tradition for the small Wyoming town where we lived.

I remember the boxes stacked in a huge pyramid reaching skyward. For a small boy standing at the base and looking upward, the scene took me away. I could only imagine the boxes when lit. What a monumental blaze that would be!

That's when it happened—a loud roar . . . confusion . . . boxes flying everywhere . . . panic . . . pain . . . tears.

I don't remember seeing the truck or even feeling the contact as the driver smashed through the boxes and into me, standing on the other side. The vehicle hit the left side of my body and sent me flying through the air. Landing was even worse. I came down hard on my right shoulder, and blistering pain surged through my body.

My brother helped me to my feet. His instinct was to stand me up. Clothes torn and face dirty, I held my arm. My shoulder screamed with pain at the slightest movement. I never learned who hit me or why, except that it was likely some student out to have a great time driving through the boxes, unaware that someone was on the other side.

My brother wanted to get me home as fast as possible. That meant walking through the cemetery, for me an unimaginable fear on top of what had already happened. Fortunately I was rescued by my sister and her boyfriend and was soon at the hospital getting treatment. I survived with a broken collarbone and a lot of bruising. However, that moment of fear was forever etched in my heart and mind.

Since then I have experienced a dozen or more different types of fear: fear of heights, failure, loss, embarrassment, financial ruin, rejection, and the fear of having my many flaws exposed. Here's what I know about fear: it paralyzes! Fear robs its host of peace, confidence, and sound judgment.

Paralyzing Fear

Gideon knew something about paralyzing fear. He lived at a time when fear ran rampant throughout Israel. Every year the Midianites swarmed into Israel, taking crops, livestock, and everything else in sight, devastating the land and leaving it empty. The Israelites endured these hostile invasions for seven years, learning to cope with the conditions.

> The sons of Israel did what was evil in the sight of the Lord; and the Lord gave them into the hands of Midian seven years. The power of Midian prevailed against Israel. Because of Midian the sons of Israel made for themselves the dens which were in the mountains and the caves and the strongholds. For it was when Israel had sown, that the Midianites would come up with the Amalekites and the sons of the east and go against them. So they would camp against them and destroy the produce of the earth as far as Gaza, and leave no sustenance in Israel as well as no sheep, ox, or donkey. For they would come up with

their livestock and their tents, they would come in like locusts for number, both they and their camels were innumerable; and they came into the land to devastate it. So Israel was brought very low because of Midian, and the sons of Israel cried to the Lord. (Judg. 6:1–6)

Now we see why Gideon feared. He had witnessed, firsthand and repeatedly, vast enemy hordes tearing up his land and destroying his crops. But God has a way of working in all things, even in one man's fearful heart.

O Valiant Warrior

"The angel of the Lord came and sat under the oak that was in Ophrah, which belonged to Joash the Abiezrite as his son Gideon was beating out wheat in the wine press in order to save it from the Midianites" (Judg. 6:11). Note that our messed up man is threshing wheat in a wine press for fear that he may be discovered and have his crop stolen.

It's likely a wise move but certainly motivated by fear. I love what happens next. "The angel of the Lord appeared to him and said to him, 'The Lord is with you, O valiant warrior'" (v. 12). Here's a man threshing his grain in a wine press, hiding out for fear of discovery, and God calls him "valiant warrior," everything that he appears not to be on the surface. God is like that, you know! He looks beyond the obvious to see the rugged potential.

The angel isn't lying when he calls Gideon a mighty warrior. He is simply speaking the truth of who Gideon will become. With one turn of the page, I can move to Judges 7 and find Gideon leading a small band of three hundred farmers to defeat the Midianites and the Amalekites, who "were lying in the valley as numerous as locusts; and their camels were without number, as numerous as the sand on the seashore" (v. 12). God, through the angel, chooses to address the courageous Gideon of chapter 7 instead of the fearful Gideon of chapter 6. To God, one page is no big deal! Chapter 6 Gideon will soon become chapter 7 Gideon, and that's the Gideon God's angel speaks to.

All men struggle with fear at different moments in their lives. But men want to be perceived as strong, confident, and courageous, so we rarely talk about our fears. In fact, we often don't acknowledge them unless forced. We whistle through the graveyard, pretending courage, while our knees rattle.

Let me tell you what encourages me when I'm feeling fearful. I like for Tina to address me as chapter 7 David. I may not be there yet, but it's helpful to be reminded that I'm just one page-turn away from becoming "a valiant warrior." I allow fear to sometimes paralyze me because I forget who I am, where I've come from, and who I'm destined to become. I start living chapter 6 instead of turning the page. Sometimes I need someone to turn the page for me—kind of like the angel did for Gideon.

When you speak courage into the messed up man in your life, you're turning his page. He may feel like running and cowering in a dark corner, but when you tell him, "You are not alone. You can do this! You are a strong mighty warrior! God has equipped you!" something happens: your messed up man rises from the darkness as light is shed on his potential.

Gideon didn't transition easily into a valiant warrior. It was a process. God took him through a series of experiences that stretched and matured him.

Early in chapter 7, Gideon sees his large army whittled down to a measly three hundred through a series of God-directed tests. God tells Gideon his army is too big. In an attempt to minimize it, Gideon says, "'Whoever is afraid and trembling, let him return and depart from Mount Gilead.' So 22,000 people returned, but 10,000 remained" (Judg. 7:3). Gideon was never the only one; 22,000 other men also feared. Then God commands Gideon to conduct one other test that eliminates the rest of the army except for the three hundred God intends to use.

But God doesn't just shrink the army. He counters Gideon's fear by allowing him to overhear a conversation about a vision one of the Midianite warriors dreamed. Emboldened by the dream and its interpretation, "[Gideon] bowed in worship. He returned to the camp of Israel and said, 'Arise, for the Lord has given the camp of Midian into your hands'" (v. 15).

It sometimes takes a bit of time for the reality of God's proclamation to sink into a man's heart. In the end, Gideon needed to hear about the dream. He needed one more divine reassurance to fully trust in his future. Perhaps your messed up man could benefit by hearing your dream of the future. Perhaps he needs to hear from your perspective that life isn't always going to be chapter 6. Even now, the page is turning!

What Men Fear

TINA ❦ Yes, Gideon feared. He feared or distrusted a lot of things:

+ the Midianites (Judg. 6:11)
+ God's word (v. 13)
+ his own strength (v. 15)
+ God's truth (v. 17)
+ God's leaving him again (v. 18)
+ the presence of God (vv. 22–23)
+ his own family (v. 27)
+ venturing into the Midianite camp by himself (7:9–11)

I'm not sure what makes a man fearful, but I do know when a man fears, the woman in his life has a good chance of fearing too. Though we can add other things to the following list, here are six things men commonly fear.

Authority

David feared Achish, king of Gath, and acted like a fool in front of him, pretending to be insane (1 Sam. 21:10–13). Daniel tells how the people feared Nebuchadnezzar's position of authority (Dan. 5:19). Gideon not only feared the Midianites who had the power to destroy his land, crops, animals, and overall means of survival, but he also feared the men in his household and city.

Though times are changing, most often men are still the providers in their homes. Men fear circumstances that can undermine that role. They may fear losing jobs. Or they may fear changes in their work or workplace, or working under the authority of bosses who belittle, tear down, and bully. Men fear other men (and women) who have the authority to change their lives and control them in some fashion—people with the ability to either promote or demote them.

Disrespect

When Queen Vashti refused the king's request to come and parade around in front of his drunken guests, the elders thought other women would disrespect their husbands the same way, and so they recommended removing her as queen (Esther 1:16–20).

In his book *Love and Respect*, Emerson Eggerichs says, "The male fear of contempt is dramatized in the first chapter of Esther—that wives would start to despise their husbands and defy them."[1]

Men want to feel respected; even the Lord spoke of being respected in Malachi 1:6–7. Being respected is a huge part of a man's life. The Bible recognizes this when it tells us that, just as men should love their wives, wives should respect their husbands (Eph. 5:33).

Feeling Insignificant or Inferior

When Jesus turned the tables over in the temple, the chief priests and scribes felt He usurped their authority and traditions. They became afraid of Him because of His teachings and how the people responded to Him. They feared the people might stop following their teachings and turn to Jesus and His teachings. Moved by fear, they plotted to get rid of Jesus (Mark 11:15–18).

Men do not want to look like underdogs or fools. They do not want to feel or appear inferior, as if they aren't as smart or wise as the man standing next to them. Men are natural competitors, and for that reason many of them struggle with feeling insignificant.

Failure

Of the twelve spies Moses sent to scout out the Promised Land, ten came back fearful of the task ahead. Some Israelites even wanted to quit (Num. 13–14).

Gideon likewise feared failure. "He said to [God], 'O Lord, how shall I deliver Israel? Behold, my family is the least in Manasseh, and I am the youngest in my father's house'" (Judg. 6:15).

Most men strive for success, accomplishments, and achievements. They want to feel their life matters and that they add value to their family as well as to their community, church, and world. Failure in such areas is something men fear.

Illness and Death

After Hezekiah received word he was going to die due to an illness, he fell before the Lord and wept (2 Kings 20:1–3). His story is far from the only one. Men fear sickness or infirmity could keep them from living out the rest of their days and being able to provide for their families.

Women

Men also fear women—what to say to them and what the result will be of being transparent. Men fear women's reactions. Will being open and honest with a woman get a man in trouble?

We see this in our families, our culture, and even on TV. One way I decompress is to engage in a movie. One evening, as my husband worked on a project in the next room, I snuggled up in a warm blanket on a cozy recliner and immersed myself in a Hallmark love story. You know—the kind that oozes sap and borders on cheesy. I didn't care; I was there! Blacking out everything else, I stepped into the story.

Here's the gist of the movie: one man's fear of a woman's finding out who he really was. He hid his real name as a well-known author and used a pen name instead. His contract said that at some point he needed to reveal his true character and name as a well-known celebrity. (I see heads nodding and hear voices: "I saw that movie!")

The movie climaxed. The author fell in love with the young reporter writing the story, who had no idea the man whose love she reciprocated was the famous writer. For some reason, he could not bring himself to tell her he was the author on whom she was reporting. The day of the reveal came. The two were about to come face to face. The reporter was going to find out who the author really was if he didn't do something, and fast. The tension was nerve-jangling. Suddenly I heard, "Why can't he just tell her who he is before the reveal!"

Shocked, I pressed the pause button and turned to find my husband shouting from the other room. He heard the television and found himself engrossed in the movie as well.

I laughed. Normally my husband wouldn't be caught dead watching a Hallmark movie (no offense to those men who do). "Sweetie," I said, "you need some serious man time." The messed up man in my life now says he fears Hallmark movies.

In all seriousness and aside from movies, men fear just as much as women do, and perhaps at times even more. Here is the question: How can women help men who fear? Perhaps perfect love has something to do with helping to dissolve fear.

Perfect Love

Gideon appears to have been loved, and loved well. According to Scripture, he had many wives plus one concubine, who together gave him seventy-one sons and who knows how many daughters (Judg. 8:29–32)! There was a lot of lovin' going on in that house.

Scripture does not tell us anything about those women in his life. However, can we envision children bouncing around and a house filled with female chatter? Busy—his home sounded busy.

I'm one of eleven children and grew up in a busy house. My youngest brother towers over everyone now, but at one point in his life, we all chased after him, babied him, and gave into him when he wanted something. Spoiled is what some of us called him, and perhaps still do. He's a good guy but still the baby of the family. Gideon was as well—the baby, the youngest, and given the idea that he was also the weakest (Judg. 6:15).

First John 4:18 says, "There is no fear in love; but perfect love casts out fear." I sit and ponder the question, what is perfect love? I contemplated it today while watching television. At one point during a cereal commercial, a small child woke up to see his father off to work the night shift. The father asked his son why he was up that late, and the boy responded, "I just wanted to have breakfast with you." As the commercial ended, the word *Love* appeared on the screen, as if to say, "Now that's love."[2] To a father, it might be considered *perfect* love.

Is perfect love the woman who poured her expensive perfume on the feet of Jesus? The boy who shared his meal to feed the five thousand? The woman in Joppa who cared for the widows? Do we see perfect love in those heroes of the Bible who delivered multitudes from captivity, baptized hundreds in the Jordan River, and endured beatings and prison just to share the gospel? Is perfect love the one who shares her kidney with a family member, gives his bone marrow to a stranger, or walks miles to work so the children are fed?

We kids never had much growing up, and always wished for some way to get Mom a Mother's Day gift. She is one to never say she felt cheated in life, but she was. Yet somehow in our messy world, she found ways to smile, hug, and love. One year my younger siblings and I decided to make something to give her for Mother's Day. We searched the land for flowers and looked for a beautiful vase but found neither. So we picked the prettiest weeds we could find and put them in an old mason jar full of water. We crouched down in our room and whispered, "Pass the glue." "I need the scissors!" When it was all over, we created a lovely flower crafted out of colored construction paper. Yes, we were little Leonardo da Vincis, and our writing ranked right up there with Emily Dickinson's. Mom was going to love it!

Four barefoot, dirty-faced kids stood before a worn-out mom and thrust a jar full of weeds in her face. "Happy Mother's Day!" we bellowed. She never flinched at what she held—only smiled. Yes, her face brightened, her lips curled up, and her eyes gleamed as she read:

Weeds may take the place of flowers,
A jar may take the place of a vase,
But nothing can take the place of you Mom,
We love you!
Happy Mother's Day!

Perfect love cast out all fear. We loved because Mom first loved us. Our life was full of fear, never knowing whether we would have a place to sleep that night or food on the table. And yes, we grew tired of sleeping on the floor, in the car, and at campgrounds. We didn't have the toys other children played with, nor did we know the pleasure of buying new dresses at a store until our teenage years. While on the road, using a gallon jug of water to brush our teeth or bathe was just a part of life. But one thing we seemed to understand is we were loved. Though our father sometimes instilled fear, our mother pushed it out with love.

A mother's love held us when we were in dark, scary places, washed our foreheads when fevers drenched our bodies, stitched holes in socks when cold toes slipped through, and crafted dolls out of scrap material for little girls to play with. A mother's love beat dirt and bugs out of stained, pocked mattresses found in abandoned homes so her children could have soft bedding. It put together pallets on cold, hard floors, kneaded bread dough, and cooked on a small campfire stove. Yes, perfect love cast out our fear.

Later in life, when my siblings came back home for a visit, one thing resounded amid the hustle and bustle—love. Through all our distress and fearful moments, in the end, we still loved one another. Was it perfect love? Some would say not—but what is perfect love?

God's love is perfect. God's love is made perfect in us. Without God's love we are unable to love at all, much less with perfection. I don't love as I should. Love pays a price. Love is costly. I can go to church, pat someone on the back, put an offering in the plate, and be done for the day, but to love outside of church is another story. To love when it costs me something is much harder. When I have to lay aside my work to help another, it costs. If I rummage through my pantry and give the things I love to eat rather than the things I don't like, it costs. When I find time to sit and listen to another person's issues, it costs. Suddenly the focus is no longer about my day, but helping another. Perfect love is nonjudgmental and mature; it's loving when we don't feel like loving. It's something none of us has arrived at but is a goal to keep pressing toward.

Perfect Love
Loves when we don't feel like it
Loves without punishment
Loves beyond our ability
Loves to cast out fear
Loves to completion

Scripture says that perfect love casts out fear. What kind of love does that? Scripture refers to it in the Greek as *agape* love: a love that is given sacrificially. It is not a feeling or emotion but an act. The only way we can love this way is through the Holy Spirit, through God. God is love and when we abide in Him, we find the ability to love.

We often connect love with our emotions, but this kind of love talks about moving into action. Agape is not the kind of sentimental love you have for your children, husband, or friend. It is sacrificial love.

The Greek word for *perfect* is *teleios*, meaning "brought to its end, finished."[3] Perfect love, then, is the kind of love that sees something through to the very end. It sees potential, it sees promise, and it sees perfection. A telescope sees beyond normal eyesight. A telephone hears beyond normal hearing. A telegraph allows you to communicate beyond normal distances. "Tele-love" is perfect love that loves beyond normal restraints.

Let's read the rest of 1 John 4:18: "There is no fear in love; but perfect love casts out fear, because fear involves punishment, and the one who fears is not perfected in love."

Wow—is John saying that when we love there should be no fear because fear and perfect love do not mix? Kind of like water and oil? We cannot love perfectly if we have fear. And when we do love with perfection, fear is dissolved.

Envision standing on a large, dark stage with scary things lurking in the background. Your heart races and your knees wobble. And then, slowly, a spotlight moves over you, enveloping you, chasing the darkness away, casting fear away. You feel the heat like a warm beam. The light is love. You feel it—see it—want to stay near it. If someone took the spotlight away after you experienced it, that would feel cruel and callous, wouldn't it?

John tells us to love without fear.

Let's sum it up. We cannot love perfectly and still have fear. Oh, we can love something or someone and experience fear, but if we love *perfectly* (to completion, to the end)—well, then fear flees.

Building Valiant Warriors

"Gideon didn't transition easily into a valiant warrior," Dave wrote earlier, and it's worth repeating. "It was a process. God took him through a series of experiences that stretched and matured him."

God chose to prove Himself to Gideon over and over again, because He understood something: Gideon lived his life in fear. God wanted to change Gideon from a fear-filled man to a solid soldier.

Step One: Revelation

God's first step in building a great warrior in Gideon was to reveal Himself. An angel visited Gideon and said, "The Lord is with you, O valiant warrior." Gideon's response: "O my lord, if the Lord is with us, why then has all this happened to us?" Have we said those words? Gideon asked for a sign and brought an offering to the Lord. The angel of the Lord caused supernatural fire to consume the offering, and the angel himself disappeared. At that moment Gideon realized he was in the presence of God (Judges 6:11–24).

In order for God to transform men and women, they must first recognize God's presence; acknowledge He's there—in all things. It's not a matter of if or when, but God *is* revealing Himself to you. Don't allow your circumstance to cloud your vision. Colossians says, "For by Him all things were created . . . visible and invisible. . . . He is before all things and in Him all things hold together" (1:16–17).

Step Two: Equipping

God's second step in warrior building involved pouring out His Holy Spirit: "The Spirit of the Lord came upon Gideon; and he blew a trumpet," rallying the Israelites (Judg. 6:34). The Holy Spirit gives us strength to do anything. He helps us in our weakness (Rom. 8:26). Gideon was suddenly surrounded by courage, zeal, and power. After accomplishing a great feat of tearing down false idols, he was now ready to help deliver his country.

Even Jesus said He could do nothing without the Father's help (John 5:19). Gideon became filled with the Spirit, and with the Spirit came the ability to rise up as a valiant warrior. Gideon was only able to receive his warrior mentality from being in the presence of God. When the Spirit of the Lord falls upon messed up men, we see fear fade and courage enter.

Step Three: Reassurance

God's third step in building a great warrior was to reassure Gideon. Sometimes in order to move from fear to courage, we need a little reassurance. Think of fathers encouraging scared little boys, "You're doing great. You've got this!"

Gideon continued to fear and need reassurance. So Gideon proposed a little test to God: he would put a wool fleece on the threshing floor. If dew settled on the fleece and the ground stayed dry, then he would know God indeed planned to deliver Israel through Gideon's leadership. God loved Gideon enough to comply.

But once wasn't enough; Gideon needed more evidence. This time the fleece would be dry and the ground wet with dew. How many times was God going to put up with this nonsense? Aren't we all saying, "Come on, Gideon! You have enough proof! You can do this!" Not

God, though. He was building confidence and courage in Gideon, the things a great warrior needs. So again He honored Gideon's request (vv. 36–40). God then gave Gideon specific instructions regarding his army, and Gideon obeyed.

In order for men to become valiant warriors, they sometimes need reassurance from God, as well as from the women in their lives.

Step Four: Confidence

Before sending Gideon into battle, God took the final step. Go spy on the Midianite camp by night, He told Gideon. He could take his servant with him if he was afraid to go alone. So Gideon and his servant snuck down to the camp, and there Gideon overheard one of the Midianites telling another about a dream he had just had. His friend interpreted its meaning: God was going to give Gideon victory in the battle.

How fitting that Gideon stumbled upon such a huge and timely revelation! Definitely no coincidence, it was not only an expression of God's love for Gideon, but it was also a moment of reassuring Gideon and filling him with confidence—a deep belief that he would succeed. He was not alone. In the end, he *would* become a great warrior!

What God did for Gideon, He wants to do for the messed up man in your life. God took Gideon through a process of turning him into a valiant warrior. Gideon had to possess a willing heart and take the steps God asked him to take. Zechariah says, "Do not despise these small beginnings, for the Lord rejoices to see the work begin" (Zech. 4:10 NLT).

Recognize those small steps. Recognize that God is revealing, equipping, reassuring, and instilling confidence. Wow—things we can do for the men in our lives.

What About Me?

What about the women who are supporting and cheering on these messed up men as they become valiant warriors? We may feel the work God does in our messed up men has nothing to do with us, but one person cannot change without it impacting another. The four small steps

Gideon took look very much the same for you. God's desire is to change not only messed up men but women who walk with them. My dear sisters, if we will look for God in all things, He will reveal Himself to us—just as He did for Gideon. With our eyes and focus upon Him, He equips. So often He hands out lifelines, but we do not recognize them because we don't see Him. When we do grab hold, He reassures, "Yes, you can do this. I'm here. I have equipped you." We step out in faith believing, understanding God is near, helping along the way. Each step instills confidence. We become strong women.

We see despair dash and joy gleam. Our Helper, the Holy Spirit, whom the Father sent, strengthens us. We hear the Lord's words, "Everything is going to be okay." "As a mother comforts her child, so will I comfort you" (Isa. 66:13 NIV). Peace falls. All is well.

Forty Years of Peace

After Gideon obeyed God, fought like a valiant warrior, and subdued the Midianites, the Israelites lived undisturbed for forty years. Peace spread throughout the countryside. People came out of their homes and out of their holes, caves, and crevices. With God's help, they walked freely and worked the land without fear.

My mother and father remained married for fifty-two years before God took my father home. I watched a mother and wife endure great loss and astounding suffering and yet continue to love one really messed up man till the day he died. She exhibited *agape* love more times than I could count. And in the end, that love triumphed. We may not have had forty years of peace in our home, but I can tell you, we did have peace.

Like Dave said, perhaps the messed up man in your life needs to hear your dream of the future. My mother had a dream that God would change my father, and He did. My mother kept turning the pages to Dad's story. Time and again I heard her say, "I'm praying. God's going to change him."

But what if my father had not allowed God to change his life? Would that have swayed my mother's love for him? I imagine my mother would have done exactly as she did—love him to the very end.

She did not always see him as a scared little boy who made terrible mistakes trying to care for himself and his family. Somehow she saw what others could not see. May we too turn the pages of our messed up man's story and come to see him as God sees him, and the way my mother saw my dad—as a valiant warrior.

Moving Beyond the Mess

1. What stood out to you in this chapter in relation to fear? What is your greatest fear?

2. Think about Gideon's background and his circumstances. What contributed to his fear? How difficult do you suppose it was for Gideon to step out with God's assignments?

3. Is there anything you can add to the list of what men fear? Compare that list to what women fear. If you feel safe sharing: What do you fear about the messed up men in your life?

4. Read Isaiah 41:10. What does it mean to you? How can this bring comfort to women who fear something in the messed up man? Read Hebrews 12:12–13. What does it say to do? How can women apply this Scripture to their lives when walking with the messed up man?

5. How difficult is it to extend *agape* love? In what areas do you struggle with loving the messed up man in your life?

6. *Moving to a healthier place:* If you had a dream for the messed up man in your life, what would it be? Make an effort this week to spend time praying over it.

May God give you the power to love unconditionally, without fear, and to the very end.

Conclusion

TINA ❀ Did you find the messed up man in your life in these chapters? Is he a Saul? Perhaps you might say he's like Peter, Samson, or Elijah. And maybe he's all of these men on any given day.

Did you notice a common thread in these chapters? All men mess up and no man is perfect, not even the men who walked with Jesus. Yet so many of the men we spoke of became great heroes of the Bible and learned incredible lessons. Moses did something he thought he could never do—help God deliver a multitude held captive for more than four hundred years. David learned to pray, repent, and call out to God. Solomon built the temple of the Lord and became the wisest king in Scripture. Elijah came to a greater understanding of God and himself. Job found more strength than he imagined. Nebuchadnezzar learned humility. Gideon learned to depend upon God, defeat a great army, and find courage. Peter grew in consistency, performing miracles, preaching the gospel, and enduring great hardships in the process. And the demoniac found freedom.

When I was a little girl I wanted nothing more than for my messed up dad to get himself together—to find freedom. I could not see that my father had no idea how to turn his life around. As I look back, I have no doubt he contemplated how to make a change. Deep inside, he was a wonderful, caring man who loved his family. But strongholds ruled his life, sin kept him chained, and addiction bound his will and desire to change. I lost hope more times than I could count.

Perhaps you have given up—lost hope. You've turned your eyes and heart away from the messed up men in your life. You've said the words,

"He'll never change!" But sister, let me remind you that God is much bigger than your emotions, thoughts, or outlook on the future.

Not until my father fell to his knees and said, "I can't do this anymore," did he find the courage to change. What a glorious man there was beneath his hard shell! Surrender your aches to God, and let God work on bringing the messed up man to his knees.

As I write, the song "Be Thou My Vision" is playing in my office, sending a sweet feeling through my soul.

> Be Thou my vision, O Lord of my heart;
> Naught be all else to me, save that Thou art.
> Thou my best thought, by day or by night,
> Waking or sleeping, Thy presence my light.
>
> Be Thou my wisdom, and Thou my true word;
> I ever with Thee and Thou with me, Lord;
> Thou my great Father, I Thy true son;
> Thou in me dwelling, and I with Thee one.
>
> Be Thou my battle shield, sword for the fight;
> Be Thou my dignity, Thou my delight;
> Thou my soul's shelter, Thou my high tower:
> Raise Thou me heavenward, O power of my power.
>
> High King of heaven, my victory won,
> May I reach heaven's joys, O bright heaven's sun!
> Heart of my own heart, whatever befall,
> Still be my vision, O Ruler of all.

There's a lot of asking and soul searching throughout this song. Here's the question: What have you asked God for? Wisdom, truth, strength, shelter, courage? What have you asked the Ruler of all to do in your life? Bring comfort, peace, joy, delight? In your messed up man's life? Heal, restore, forgive, release, change?

I know that when times get tough with the messed up man, the easier route is to brush him aside—forget about him. He's made his bed; let him lie in it. But may I encourage you to keep God as your vision. When we turn our vision away from God, we do not see what God sees; we only see what Satan or the world throws at us. But with God as our vision, we stay the course. We come to see the good in messed up men rather than heed what other people and our own hurtful experiences have to say about them. With God as our vision, we press on toward the prize. Remember, it's not about changing messed up men but walking with them and coming to see them as God sees them.

You may never see the messed up man in your life change, but through the journey you will find that your own life changes. And who knows? Perhaps the messed up man will look at your life and grab hold of those precious nuggets that lead him to make a life-altering change in his own heart—all because of your example.

With God as your vision, you, my friend, will come to a greater understanding of what it means to run the race and run it well. In the end God will say, "Well done, My good and faithful servant."

DAVE 🌾 In the early days, when this book was still an undefined idea, I took an informal poll of some of my friends, asking for their thoughts on the most pressing issues men face. I made a list of the top answers, and Tina and I began to search for biblical men who shared the same flaws. Some of those examples were easier to find than others. The process of discovering and writing about these messed up men of the Bible brought me to an early conclusion: I can see myself in each of them.

I initially intended to write this book for men to give them hope, provide instruction, and share the healing that only God can provide. We had already written two chapters when someone suggested that the book needed to be written for women. I reluctantly came to agree, and Tina and I changed our focus to "seeing your man through the eyes of God." My challenge became to write a book about men that was addressed to women. I have plenty to say to men; I just wasn't sure I had much to say to the ladies.

What I've tried to do with my words is help you make sense of your messed up man. I want you to understand that his issues, no matter how dysfunctional, are common, at least to some extent, to all men. I hope you see that the men whom God used throughout the pages of Scripture were also messed up in a variety of ways.

Tina told me consistently throughout the writing process that I should just put on paper what I would tell you if you were sitting in my office sharing about your messed up man. I have had many of those conversations over the years regarding husbands, sons, fathers, brothers, coworkers, boyfriends, etc.

Here's what I tell everyone every time.

You are not alone. You are not the first one to deal with this, and you will not be the last. The reason Tina and I are pointing out the issues that these biblical characters possess is to help you recognize that God has been calling and working through messed up men since the beginning of the world.

You can't fix the issue. Everything in you may scream that you need to somehow control your man and your circumstances. But control will not work. Your man will work on his issues when the pain of staying the same is greater than the pain of changing. This doesn't mean that you do nothing, but it does mean you don't try to control the storm.

I learned the "Twelve Steps" firsthand in Celebrate Recovery. Let's apply a brief summary of the first three steps to your man.

Step One: You can't control him or his behavior.

Step Two: Only God has the power to change him and his behavior.

Step Three: Make a continual decision to turn your man over to the care of God.

With those three steps in mind, allow me to offer a few practical guidelines for your journey.

Set appropriate boundaries to keep yourself safe and healthy. Don't hesitate to seek out guidance from your minister, a counselor, or a trusted mentor. It may be helpful to seek guidance from a professional to whom you can turn with your questions. If you feel you are in danger, please find help immediately.

Don't waste the hurt. Let this situation be an opportunity to work on your own issues. I would recommend you find a Celebrate Recovery program in a church near you. Celebrate Recovery is a Christ-centered recovery program found in more than 20,000 churches nationwide. Find a group and read more about Celebrate Recovery at www.celebrate recovery.com.

Find a trusted female friend with whom you can share your story honestly. My friend and counselor, Tom Pals, describes the difference between privacy and secrecy. He says, "Someone needs to know everything, but not everyone needs to know everything." I always caution people to be extremely careful with whom they share their story. They must have a proven track record of being trustworthy.

Get closer to God. I've found that God is never as close as He is in times of my brokenness and despair. There was a time when I blindly believed that God only used perfect people. My own efforts to live up to that human perfection only left me frustrated and hopeless. Throughout my life, I've become acquainted with the diverse group of messed up men and wounded women found in the Bible whom God calls His friends. "Draw near to God and He will draw near to you" (James 4:8).

Let me close with a prayer:

Father, bless the precious life who is reading these words at this very moment. Come close to her, hold her, and sing your love songs over her. Wipe away her tears, restore her wounded soul, and strengthen her broken spirit. Whatever is in her past, her present, and her future is given to You for Your care. We ask for healing for her messed up man and for You to take control and provide real-life change. Bring faith. Bring hope. Bring love. In Jesus's name. Amen.

Notes

Chapter 1. Peter

1. Charles Colson and Nancy Pearcey, *How Now Shall We Live?* (Carol Stream, IL: Tyndale, 1999), 379.
2. *Merriam-Webster*, s.v. "authenticity," accessed October 16, 2015, http://www.merriam-webster.com/dictionary/authenticity.
3. Paul references Peter's wife traveling with him in 1 Corinthians 9:5. Cephas is Peter.
4. *Merrian-Webster*, s.v. "reverence," accessed October 16, 2015, http://www.merriam-webster.com/dictionary/reverence.

Chapter 2. Nebuchadnezzar

1. Quoted by Scott Carson, "Who Wants to Be #2?" (sermon), May 2000, http://www.sermoncentral.com/sermons/who-wants-to-be-2-scott-carson-sermon-on-jesus-teachings-35269.asp.
2. C. S. Lewis, *Mere Christianity*, revised and amplified ed. (HarperCollins, 2001), 124.
3. Ibid., 126.
4. Sarah Young, *Jesus Calling* (Nashville: Thomas Nelson, 2004), 361.
5. Michelle Kugler, psychotherapist, personal email to the authors, January 2014.

Chapter 3. Saul

1. Les Parrott III, *The Control Freak* (Wheaton, IL: Tyndale, 2000), 21–33.
2. Herbert Lockyer, *All the Women of the Bible*, "Ahinoam No. 1" (Grand Rapids: Zondervan, 1988), 29.

3. Bill Johnson, *Strengthen Yourself in the Lord: How to Release the Hidden Power of God in Your Life* (Shippensburg, PA: Destiny Image Publishers, 2007), 67.

4. Debra Evans, *Six Qualities of Women of Character: Life-Changing Examples of Godly Women* (Grand Rapids: Zondervan, 1996), 80.

5. Jennifer Strickland, *Beautiful Lies* (Eugene, OR: Harvest House, 2013), 16.

Chapter 4. Moses

1. Neil T. Anderson and Rich Miller, *Getting Anger Under Control: Overcoming Unresolved Resentment, Overwhelming Emotions, and the Lies Behind Anger* (Eugene, OR: Harvest House, 2002), 82.

2. The name has been changed.

Chapter 5. Job

1. Jerry Bridges, *Trusting God Even When Life Hurts* (Carol Stream, IL: NavPress, 1988).

2. Hebrew Lexicon :: Strong's H1288, *barak*, Blue Letter Bible, accessed May 7, 2015, http://www.blueletterbible.org/lang/lexicon/lexicon.cfm ?strongs=H1288.

3. Francis I. Andersen, *Job*, Tyndale Old Testament Commentaries (Carol Stream, IL: IVP Academic, 2008), 93 (emphasis in original).

4. Bible History Online, *International Standard Bible Encyclopedia*, s.v. "Mephibosheth," accessed May 7, 2015, http://www.bible-history.com/isbe /M/MEPHIBOSHETH/.

5. Helen Keller, *The World I Live In and Optimism* (Mineola, NY: Dover Publications, 2009), 88.

Chapter 6. Elijah

1. A Christ-centered recovery program. Visit their Website at http://www .celebraterecovery.com/.

2. Dictionary.com, s.v. "knitted," accessed May 7, 2015, http://dictionary .reference.com/browse/knitted.

3. John C. Maxwell, *Talent Is Never Enough: Discover the Choices That Will Take You Beyond Your Talent* (Nashville: Thomas Nelson, 2007), 24.

4. *Merriam-Webster*, s.v. "understand," accessed October 16, 2015, http://www.merriam-webster.com/dictionary/understand.

Chapter 7. Solomon

1. Marlena Graves, "'He's Just Not a Spiritual Leader,' and Other Christian Dating Myths," November 19, 2012, http://www.christianitytoday.com/women/2012/november/hes-just-not-spiritual-leader-and-other-christian-dating.html?paging=off.
2. *Oxford Dictionary*, s.v. "spiritual," accessed October 16, 2015, http://www.oxforddictionaries.com/us/definition/american_english/spiritual.
3. Patricia A. Halbert, ed., *I Wish I Knew That: U.S. Presidents: Cool Stuff You Need to Know*, by the editors of *Reader's Digest* (New York: The Reader's Digest Assoc., 2012), n.p.
4. The 700 Club, "Dr. Henry Cloud: Leading with Boundaries," Guest Bio, accessed May 7, 2015, http://www.cbn.com/700club/guests/bios/Henry_Cloud_051313.aspx.

Chapter 8. David

1. Michelle Kugler, in an email message to the author, February 15, 2015.
2. Ibid.
3. *Merriam-Webster*, s.v. "encourage," accessed October 21, 2015, http://www.merriam-webster.com/dictionary/encourage.
4. Geoff Gorsuch, *Brothers!: Calling Men into Vital Relationships* (Colorado Springs: Navpress, 1994), 14.
5. Gary Smalley and John Trent, *The Blessing: Giving the Gift of Unconditional Love and Acceptance* (New York: Simon & Schuster, 1986).

Chapter 9. Judas

1. *Merriam-Webster*, s.v. "accountable," accessed October 21, 2015, http://www.merriam-webster.com/dictionary/accountable.
2. Beth Moore, *So Long, Insecurity: You've Been a Bad Friend to Us* (Carol Stream, IL: Tyndale), 7.
3. Robert South, "I Have Called You Friends," in *The Book of Jesus*, ed. Calvin Miller (New York: Simon & Schuster, 1996), 180.

Chapter 10. Samson

1. Fred and Brenda Stoeker, *Every Heart Restored: A Wife's Guide to Healing in the Wake of a Husband's Sexual Sin* (Colorado Springs: WaterBrook, 2010), 49.
2. Ibid., 52.
3. Used by permission. Mark R. Laaser, *The Secret Sin: Healing the Wounds of Sexual Addiction*, Lifelines for Recovery Series (Grand Rapids: Zondervan, 1992), excerpted at http://www.addiction-help.org/?page_id=27.
4. PR Newswire, "Is the Internet Bad for Your Marriage? Online Affairs, Pornographic Sites Playing Greater Role in Divorces," November 14, 2002,   http://www.prnewswire.com/news-releases/is-the-internet-bad -for-your-marriage-online-affairs-pornographic-sites-playing-greater -role-in-divorces-76826727.html.

Chapter 11. The Demoniac

1. J. R. R. Tolkien, *The Hobbit; or, There and Back Again*, rev. ed. (New York: Ballantine, 1966), 115.
2. Beth Moore, *Praying God's Word: Breaking Free from Spiritual Strongholds* (Nashville: B & H, 2009), 128.

Chapter 12. Gideon

1. Emerson Eggerichs, *Love and Respect: The Love She Most Desires; The Respect He Desperately Needs* (Nashville: Thomas Nelson, 2004), 57.
2. "Ad's tribute to night shift workers leaves KLG, Hoda in tears," accessed May 7, 2015, http://www.today.com/parents/3rd-shift-cheerios-ad-leaves -klg-hoda-tears-2D80160197.
3. Greek Lexicon :: Strong's G5046, *teleios*, Blue Letter Bible, accessed May 7, 2015, http://www.blueletterbible.org/lang/lexicon/lexicon.cfm ?strongs=G5046.

Acknowledgments

TINA ✻ God, at this moment, is saying, "Phew!" In truth, He never tired of my outbursts of "I can't do this!" The many times I called out, "Give me something, God! Just give me something!" God embraced me as I cried a mound of tears over these chapters, rubbed my temples raw, and spent countless hours diving into the lives of these messed up men. In truth, all God cared about was comforting me and giving me the courage to move forward with this project. Thank you, God—my biggest believer.

To My Messed Up Men

A hug goes out to my dad, who passed away several years ago. I miss you every day, and I loved seeing your life change.

A warm embrace to my hubby, Dave, who came up with the idea for this book. I loved digging into the chapters with you and watching God work in your life—the same God who turns messes into grace-filled moments.

Thank you, my sons Jaren and Zach, for enduring a crazy momma who's trying to live in an all-male household. You are beams of light that keep me smiling. I love you both.

A big hug to the rest of the men in my life—my brothers, uncles, cousins, and friends. I've seen your messes, and I've seen your changes— and I adore you so much.

To the Women Who Love Messed Up Men

To one of my dearest friends, Dena—thank you for teaching me so much about writing and for always being available to help when I need it. I'm so glad we literally live next door.

Gloria, my dear friend, thank you for always being there. I miss my yard sale Saturday morning breakfast buddy!

The women of Grace River Church—how precious you are. I miss you all.

Thank you ladies (and men) of Tolar Baptist Church for your encouragement and prayers. You've blessed me beyond my dreams.

To my readers—thank you for taking the time to share your thoughts. Dena, Kristie, Debbie, and Michelle, I loved your feedback, and thank you for your insight on the book.

Many thanks to all the women in my life. To those who've picked up my book *Wounded Women of the Bible* and found hope; to the Bible study leaders and those who've sat in on my Bible study classes; to the prison ministry leaders, support group leaders, life groups, mentors, and friends who sit with one another to study God's Word and read anything I've written—thank you, all of you, for your encouraging words, for walking with hurting women, and for blessing beyond measure.

And to those women who email me their deepest hurts and openly share tragic life moments: I promise to pray for you. I feel honored you would reach out to me for prayer or counsel and trust me with your wounds. Keep pressing on. God is never far away.

To the Special Women in My Life

Mom, sisters, sisters-in-law, aunts, cousins, and nieces—thank you for getting excited about the little things in my life and for bellowing about the big ones. I love you gals.

A special and huge thank you to my precious cousin, Sarah. Without your help this book would have been a mess! Thank you for the long hours of editing and helpful insight.

To Those Who Care

Word Serve Literary Agency, I'm grateful for your work. Thank you for the feedback and for working hard to get this book noticed.

Thank you, Kregel Publications, for your work on my last book and for what you and your team have done with this one. Thank you, Steve, Dawn, Bob, Sarah, and others for the many hours of work on this book. I learned so much!

To the bookstores who've allowed me to come into your store— thank you!

Above all, may God receive the glory for what He will do with this book!

DAVE ❦ I've come to understand that God calls the broken and the bruised and that He demonstrates His strength through courageous acts of renewal. I'm encouraged that Jesus said the poor in spirit (the spiritually bankrupt) would inherit the same reward as those who are persecuted for doing the right things. Both receive the kingdom of heaven (Matt. 5:3, 10). I am grateful to my Lord Jesus for making all things new.

I am indebted to my coauthor and companion for life, Tina. I'll never forget the moment I first laid eyes on you that summer day in Wyoming, when you first stepped off the church bus. We were young and naive and could have never imagined the difficult road we would travel together. I can honestly say that I love you today more than ever, having had the experience of sharing our lives together—for richer, for poorer, in sickness and in health (actually, I'm still waiting to share in the "richer" part). Thanks for pushing me to write and for picking up the slack when I had nothing to say. You will always be my favorite author, my favorite worship leader, and my favorite breakfast buddy.

My sons, Jaren and Zach, are the joy of my heart. Thanks to both of you for the way your lives demonstrate such strong character. I couldn't be prouder.

Thanks to Ken Datson, Tom Pals, Amos Lawrence, Gary Clyma, and Martin Castro. You each walked with me through a difficult time, and I am indebted.

I was overwhelmed by the love and blessing I experienced at Grace

River Church, serving as your pastor for five wonderful years. All of your faces are in my mind as I write. I wish I could include all of your names, for you are altogether the ocean of love on which my ship has sailed.

Thanks to all of the churches that have allowed me to serve them, beginning with FBC in Camden, Tennessee, which called me as a college student to serve as a summer youth worker way back in 1984. Thirty years later, I'm excited to be starting a new journey with a great church in Tolar, Texas—Tolar Baptist Church.

I appreciate Word Serve Literary Agency and Kregel Publications for enabling this project to move forward.

There are friends who stick closer than a brother. Thanks David Mills and Mendal Kugler.

I love and appreciate my brothers and sisters: Sandy Evans, Cindy Stauffenberg, and Mike Samples. I'm glad that we're getting together every year. I've needed that.

God saw fit to take my mom home in 2005. She went quickly and none of us had the opportunity to say good-bye or express our love. I miss her and wish I could spend another day with her on this side. My mom was an amazing woman who loved life! She had a great sense of humor and a wonderful laugh. I miss you, Mom!

Dad, you've shown me that it's okay to struggle and that we're not defined by failure. I love you so much, and I am grateful that we have been able to share so many wonderful moments together. You are one of God's heroes who will certainly have a special place in heaven. Everything I know about pastoring I learned by watching you. Thanks for being my dad!

About the Authors

Tina Samples

Tina is an award-winning author, speaker, worship leader, and music therapist. She lives in Granbury, Texas, with her husband, Dave, who is the lead pastor of Tolar Baptist Church. Together they have two gifted sons, Jaren and Zach, and one granddaughter.

Wounded Women of the Bible: Finding Hope When Life Hurts, coauthored with Dena Dyer, received the 2014 Golden Scroll Award for nonfiction book of the year. Tina's other publishing credits include *It's a God Thing: Stories to Help You Experience The Heart of God*; *True Stories of Extraordinary Answers to Prayer: Unexpected Answers*; *True Stories of Extraordinary Answers to Prayer: In Times of Change*; *Angels, Miracles, and Heavenly Encounters: Real Life Stories of Supernatural Events*; and *The One Year Life Verse Devotional*. She has also contributed to *The Secret Place* devotional magazine, as well as to *Quiet Hour* magazine. Her articles about music therapy have appeared in the *Colorado Baptist News*.

Tina also had the privilege of being cast for two years as a singer in the musical *TEXAS*, in Canyon, Texas, and for two seasons in *The Promise*, in Glen Rose, Texas. Find out more about Tina at www.tinasamples.com, and follower her on Twitter (@tinasamples), Facebook (www.facebook.com/TinaSamplesAuthor), and Pinterest (www.pinterest.com/tinasamples).

Dave Samples

Dave is a pastor, teacher, author, and church planter. He is a native Texan who resides in Granbury, Texas. Currently, he's lead pastor at

Tolar Baptist Church in Tolar, Texas. Dave has held numerous denominational leadership positions and has spoken for a variety of organizations including the Gospel Music Association in Estes Park, Colorado.

Dave has a Master of Divinity Degree with Biblical Languages from Southwestern Baptist Theological Seminary, Fort Worth, Texas.

Dave has served as a chaplain in the US Navy, as well as chaplain for local fire and police departments. In 2008, he was nominated as Windsor, Colorado, Person of the Year in recognition of his efforts to provide disaster relief following a devastating tornado.

Dave and Tina have two sons, Jaren and Zach, and one granddaughter, Abigail.

You can find David online at www.davesamples.blogspot.com, or link with him via Facebook or Twitter (@davesamples).

A Message from Tina & Dave

Dear Friends,

Sometimes life is challenging. We want you to know we're here if you need us. We have the incredible privilege of ministering to broken and hurting people all across the United States. Send an email—we write back and on occasion pick up the phone for a visit. Funny thing is, after, "Hello, can you pray with me?" a bond is formed and a new friend found.

Here are a few things you might want to know:

+ We will skype your intro or closing Bible study class free of charge (if you're doing our study or *Wounded Women of the Bible*).
+ Keep us in mind for conferences, retreats, events, and speaking engagements. David also speaks at revivals.
+ Aside from speaking, Tina leads worship. Together we make a great team but are also asked to attend individual events.

Our deepest prayer is that you not sit one more second in a puddle of pain. There is a great big ray of light waiting for you to step its way. A light that brings warmth, freedom, and gleaming hope. You can do this. Together, we can do this.

Blessings!

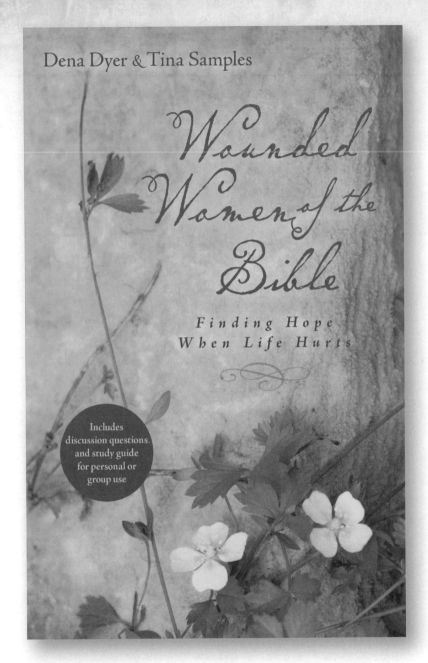

Dena Dyer & Tina Samples

Wounded Women of the Bible

Finding Hope When Life Hurts

Includes discussion questions and study guide for personal or group use

The healing takes place when
we realize we are not alone.